Deep insights delivered croissant-style. Another helping, please.

— THE **GUY WHO IS ALWAYS AT STARBUCKS**

Start to finish on a plane ride….

— THE **GROUNDED EXEC**

Slap my forehead. Made a few of these mistakes. Wish I had read this book earlier.

— **NEWBIE NO MORE**

*I made these reviews up… no seriously; I did.*

# 11 CEO HABITS - WAKE UP THE CEO WITHIN YOU

*This book uses the simplest words possible. But not always.*

*It contains no padding or fluff. Read less, reflect more.*

*Read with inner wisdom. It knows what you must know.*

*The reader reads to recall, not learn. Can anything be taught, except
what the heart already knows?*

*The target reader for this book is The Hands-On CEO, The Conscientious Manager, The Grayscale Employee, The Noble Newbie, The Intelligent Intern.*

---

## THE HANDS-ON CEO

The Hands-On CEO dismantles hierarchy if it blocks visibility into the guts of the company.

The Hands-On CEO jumps into the driving seat and stays there.

He does weird things. Like meeting every candidate slated to be hired. And mingles with interns.

## THE CONSCIENTIOUS MANAGER

The manager is in the middle of the organizational hierarchy. She is criticized both ways — when she **behaves** like a manager and when she **doesn't behave** like a manager.

The manager was once a star salesperson or one-man team — achieving targets and working alone. As a manager, he follows orders and gives orders, meets targets and assigns targets, works alone and with others. He has new KPIs — inspire the team, drive results through others, build a personal brand. It is a tough balancing act.

## THE GRAYSCALE EMPLOYEE

The employee whose words evoke mixed emotions — was that a compliment, a criticism or a warning?

The grayest of them play a zero-sum game — when you lose, he wins.

## THE NEWBIE

The endearing first-time-on-a-full-time-job soul.

Doesn't know what attitude to bring to work.

Whatever he does seems to be wrong.

The grayscale employees ensure newbies earn their stripes through a trial by fire.

# THE INTELLIGENT INTERN

The leaders of the future. Our hope and legacy for a better world.

*The throat clearing and silly stuff about why I wrote this book is at the end of the book.*

*The people who helped me write this book do not wish to be named. So it's just me who takes the flak.*

# CONTENTS

# PART I

THE CEO
HABITS

# CHAPTER 1
# CEO HABITS - HIDDEN IN PLAIN SIGHT

*You see power, leadership, excellence, not the habits!*

CEO habits are hidden in plain sight.

You do not see these, and it's not your fault. Because the *results* — power, leadership, excellence — grab the spotlight.

Managers[1], newbies[2] and interns[3] are led to believe they must be leaders, but workplace culture often penalizes[4] leadership behaviors at lower levels of the hierarchy. Organizations demand leaders, yet reward followers. The manager, newbie and intern sits on the fence[5] forlorn — unable to choose between toeing the line[6] and being an entrepreneurial, disruptive[7] presence. If this is you, read on.

CEO habits are the missing link, the glue that makes leadership actions stick, and create value for the organization.

CEO habits appear to be traits[8], but are *habits*. The CEO cultivates these habits through mindful application, till they become a part of the personality.

As a manager, newbie and intern, build CEO habits as a foundation for personal mastery and professional excellence.

*Gonna rock the world with CEO habits!*

*Up next* 👉 *CEO Habits — Standing on the shoulders of giants.*

The CEO seeks giants.

# CHAPTER 2
## STANDING ON THE SHOULDERS OF GIANTS

## CEO HABITS
# STANDING ON THE SHOULDERS OF GIANTS

Find a giant. Stand on shoulder.

### WHAT'S A GIANT?

A giant is a source of knowledge, expertise and situational power. The giant is easy to access. When giants perch you on the shoulder, you see further and go further.

## WHY CALL THEM GIANTS?

They are giants because they share deep expertise and ease your path, expecting nothing in return.

## IT CAN'T BE SO EASY. WHAT'S THE CATCH?

Giants have things to do, they do not wait for dwarfs, and they don't serve dwarfs. The learning must be on the giant's terms.

## WHO ARE THESE GIANTS?

*Become a giant by utilizing giants.*

Meet the giants — books, business connections, subject matter experts, role models, mentors, devil's advocate *aka* murder board.

The CEO seeks giants. He knows there is *always* someone who has the knowledge, expertise and power to ease his path right now.

## EVERYONE SEEKS GIANTS, RIGHT?

Sort of, but not really. Managers, newbies and interns often get on the wrong side of giants, resent them, refuse to utilize them, ignore them or treat them as cheatsheets[1]-on-demand. Sometimes, they try to dupe[2] giants into serving them. Here's how the 'dupe script' looks like.

Dwarf: I need your help

Giant: Sure, shoot!

Dwarf: I don't know how to do this…

Giant: It's easy. You can learn it in a few days or weeks. Let's get started.

Dwarf: Err, I don't have the time for that.

Giant: What do you mean?

Dwarf: I need your help to do it, not learn it.

Giant: Sure, let's work on it together.

Dwarf: Err, I don't have time for that.

Giant: What do you mean?

Dwarf: I am swamped[3] in stuff. Can you do it for me? That's the help I need. You don't have to do it right now. But I have to send it out by end-of-day tomorrow.

*Giant self-destructs[4]. End of conversation.*

*The giant self-destructs after listening to a 'dupe script'*

## HERE IS ANOTHER ONE.

A lifetime ago, one of the business unit managers walked into my office.

He said, *"I am falling short on my sales targets. Can you help me?"*

I said, *"Sure, what can I do for you?"*

*"Can you get me purchase orders to meet my sales targets?"*

Took me a while to get over that one.

## WHY ARE GIANTS NOT UTILIZED?

**URGENCY** — you focus on meeting immediate needs and never find time for giants. You want fish without learning to fish[5].

*"Seriously? This can take forever. I don't have time for this."*

**GAP** — the gap between the giant's competence and self-perception of your (in)competence intimidates you. The camel sees the mountain, says OMG![6], and turns back.

*"OMG! Hear ye, I won't, I can't, and that's final!"*

**EFFORT** — you are reluctant to ascend the steep learning curve[7]. The effort takes you out of the comfort zone[8].

*"Meeting the mountain means an awful learning curve!"*

**DESIRE** — you are not hungry enough.

**UNDERVALUATION** — you don't realize the worth of a giant ready to teach you for free.

**INVISIBLE ACTIVITY** — Sales force automation[9] tools acknowledge time spent in training but not talent development[10]. Your time with giants fetches no brownie points[11].

*"Ahem! I could teach the giant a thing or two."*

**DELUSION**[12] — you believe your skill sets and abilities are adequate. In fact, you believe giants have a lot to learn from you.

**INSECURITY** — Giants could be your subordinates. You doubt that a colleague lower in the hierarchy[13] would respect you if they taught you something. (The answer is yes, they would.)

*"Life is so unfair. Hrrmph!"*

**EMOTIONS** — you envy the giant, his competence makes it worse. The camel sees the mountain and is aggrieved at its stature.

## UNLEASH THE BENEFITS OF GIANTS

To unleash the benefits of giants, here is what you need to know.

*Books are giants that never say no.*

**BOOKS** — are not human, they don't compete with you. Start with these giants. The right books will find you, jump off the screen even. Get a subscription to your favorite bookstore — Kindle, Apple, Nook, Kobo, whatever. Kindle Unlimited subscribers read most books for free. E-book reader devices and apps allow access to the thesaurus without leaving the page. Download books in the public domain for free. A curated[14] reading list appears in the concluding pages of this book. Can life get better than this?

**BUSINESS CONNECTIONS** — you've got a ton of them, but you don't use them as giants. Why? Because these are buried within business cards, rolodex[15], smart-phone directory, emails, messaging apps and

LinkedIn connections. If you don't see them, you won't use them. For heaven's sake, adopt a CRM[16] tool. The sales person's dislike for CRM refuses to die. You say, "*Would I give away precious contacts to the organization, so they kick me out at a moment's notice?*" Well, then get a single CRM license for *personal* use. Bitrix24[17] offers a free version with features that make you hum a tune.

Then start a blog and post on LinkedIn to build credibility with business connections. Go easy on the hashtags[18]. Meaning, avoid overuse of hashtags in a post. Share your posts with relevant business connections. Don't pitch. *Just. Stay. Connected.*

Send personalized email[19] to business connections once a year. Document management[20] software lets you personalize emails by inserting the recipient's name to a generic draft. If possible, include a memory, market news or trivia applicable to the recipient. Consistency is the key. Business connections may ignore the annual email as a marketing tactic[21]. Eventually they will realize it is not a tactic, it is who you are.

You need the situational power[22] and specialized knowledge of your business connections. When you stay connected, it is easy to enlist their support. Let business connections see you as more than a generic season's greeting message.

**SUBJECT MATTER EXPERTS**[23] — are people who know a lot about a subject. They know 'how to do' something really well. *How do you recognize a subject matter ex-*

*pert?* They are often your colleagues. Subject matter experts know how to facilitate transfer of knowledge. They are happy to make time for you if you are willing to learn.

**ROLE MODELS**[24] — are living or deceased individuals that you admire. Study the value framework[25] of the person you admire and use it to create a personal development roadmap[26].

**MENTORS**[27] — are persons who hone your talent. Mentors choose you. When this happens, it seems a soul connection. The relationship hums along with the least effort. Be grateful and make the mentoring experience well worth the mentor's time. Pay it forward. Develop the attributes that would make you a mentor to future generations.

**DEVIL'S ADVOCATE**[28] *AKA* **MURDER BOARD**[29] — are friends, family and colleagues who pick holes in your ideas, solutions, and projects. Their minds naturally zoom in to the weak links. They are the proof-readers who spot every typo. The devil's advocates are like gold, even the worst of them. Treat their inputs as real world objections. Work on the value proposition of your idea, solution and project accordingly.

Not every critic is fit to be the devil's advocate. Separate fault-finding inputs from constructive criticism.

The CEO is not shy to stand on the shoulders of giants. I have a murder board that has proven its credentials over time. An idea sent to them comes back with an analysis. That would cost me money and time if I hired consultants.

Use giants to see further, go further.

---

*Up next* ☛ *CEO Habits — Winning with Words*

Winning with words builds personal equity.

# CHAPTER 3
# WINNING WITH WORDS

## CEO HABITS

# WINNING WITH WORDS

Stop. Don't think of flowery language or formula phrases.

Think gentleman's word[1], elevator pitch[2], great comebacks[3] and the book Lifescripts[4].

## THE GENTLEMAN'S WORD

The gentleman's word is equal to a signed agreement. It means you do what you say.

The CEO takes his words seriously. The gentleman's word is a habit; a cornerstone of personal brand identity.

As a manager, newbie and intern, have you failed to keep your word at times? Take heart.

Blogger and Style Advisor Antonio Centeno[5] describes his journey towards keeping the word. He says, *"In one case, it was a full year before I made good on my word… it felt horrible."* Read the blog article A Man's Word Is His Bond — 4 Tips To Keep Your Promises[6]

## ELEVATOR PITCH

Elevator pitch is a 30 second description of your idea, product, company or yourself. It sparks the listener's interest and leads to longer conversations, sales conversions, or a job offer.

The CEO has an elevator pitch to describe his company, ideas, job, family, kids, cat, dog, everything. He uses it to save time and uncover opportunities.

As a manager, newbie and intern, you manage products, brands, organizational equity and career. If you don't have an elevator pitch, that's not good news. If you can't **KISS** (Keep It Short, Stupid) at sales prospect meetings, kiss opportunities goodbye.

*"I will be talking to myself till the cows come home."*

The elevator pitch opens windows of opportunity and gives you a foot-in-the-door. It hooks the listener's attention. Blogger and Resume Expert Michael Tomaszewski[7] says, "Without attention, you might as well talk to the hand." Read the blog article How to Write an Elevator Pitch[8].

You will find great stuff on the web by using the search keyword '**elevator pitch examples**'.

## THE GREAT COMEBACK

A great comeback is a clever reply to a hurtful comment. The person making the hurtful comment may be a peer, colleague or business associate. They may cloak words as humor or contextual statements. The true intention is to embarrass you or put you down.

The CEO uses 'the great comeback' to manage power dynamics. He defuses the attack and restores the professional purpose of the interaction.

If colleagues say nasty things that make you bawl your eyes out, you need a great comeback. "Why didn't I say…?" is a common regret reported by victims when they calm down and mentally replay the scenario. A great comeback could have defused the situation.

Dr. Mark Goulston[9] advises, "… don't feel blindsided and pushed off balance by a verbal bully". Read the blog article 7 Comebacks to a Verbal Bully[10].

Below are blog articles to make you laugh. Don't use these comebacks, though.

Top Ten Clean Comebacks and Roasts[11]

Top Ten Counter Comebacks To Other People's Comebacks[12]

25 Funny Ways to Say NO[13]

## LIFESCRIPTS

The book Lifescripts[14] maps 109 perplexing conversations you may encounter at the workplace.

Managers, newbies and interns are at a loss of words when confronted with difficult situations at the workplace. Use Lifescripts to control dialogue and its outcomes. The book teaches how to hold your ground across challenging scenarios and exchanges of words.

If you gain only one thing from this book, let it be this. Conversations turn out the way you want only when you control them.

Lifescripts can be read for free[15] on the Internet Archive[16]. If you buy the book, order the print edition, not the ebook[17]. As Jill Lightner[18] says, *"Place the book on an accessible shelf… so you find it when life's surprises head your way."*

Someone said, *"The pursuit of great things is ruined by a faucet leaking in the kitchen."* You cannot soar the skies when workplace conversations pin you down in despair.

The CEO wins with words and so will you.

Here is a reading list to build a winning words arsenal.

**Exactly What To Say[19] — The Magic Words For Influence And Impact.** By Phil M. Jones.

**How To Win Any Argument[20] — Without Raising Your Voice, Losing Your Cool, Or Coming To Blows.** By Robert Mayer.

---

*Up next ☛ CEO Habits — Brevity*

Brevity magnifies the power of words.

# CHAPTER 4
# BREVITY

Speak less, convey more. Make it interesting. Keep it meaningful. This is brevity.

Brevity is the skill of making it fit on a single page. It requires you to organize thoughts and words, and get to the point, quick.

## IMAGINE THE SCENARIO

*Running into the CEO on a bright, sunny morning*

You run into the CEO at the coffee machine. He asks, *"How is it going? What is your evaluation of portfolio performance this quarter?"*

The truth — it's not going well. Your line manager has scheduled an SOS meeting. How do you tell this to the CEO on a bright, sunny morning?

The CEO continues, *"Competitor XYZ has added 3 people to their team. What are they doing that we aren't?"*

You think, "Seriously, where does the CEO get his information? Is he pulling a fast one on me? What do I say?"

You can extricate yourself from this conversation with the brevity response. The brevity response is a short (and sometimes bullsh*t) script.

Try this. "Hmm, I scanned the news this morning. The global impact is reflecting on our market. However, it can be safely said that quarter performance goals must remain the same or revised in an upward direction. Certain challenges may, in fact, be opportunities in disguise. These are slated for discussion with the team. If you like, I could email you market related observations for this week."

Now escape as fast as you can (your coffee is getting cold).

## WHY DOES THE BREVITY RESPONSE WORK?

The brevity response works because you communicate energy and control in a few sentences. You started with action, mentioned the big picture and showed steadfastness to goals.

Don't believe me?

## THE ANALYSIS

**ACTION** — *I scanned the news today.*

**BIG PICTURE** — *The global impact is reflecting on our market.*

**STEADFASTNESS TO GOALS** — *It can be safely said that targets must remain the same or revised in an upward direction.*

**POSITIVE MINDSET** — *Certain problems may be opportunities in disguise.*

**Follow-through** — *These are slated for discussion with the team.*

**Diligence** — *market related observations for this week.*

You satiate the curiosity of the CEO — does (s)he know what (s)he is doing? A six-sentence paragraph gets you off the hook on a bright, sunny morning. That is brevity.

## BREVITY IS A SURVIVAL TOOL

The CEO uses brevity as a time management and survival tool.

CEOs get into trouble. Yeah, they screw up. *Leakage of company information is discovered too late. Company stocks are in free fall. Sales performance declines across the portfolio. A competitor wins several prestigious projects in a row. A white collar criminal flies out of the country undetected.*

The list goes on.

You need the skills of Houdini[1] to pull off sensational escapes from these sticky situations.

## BREVITY SCRIPT TO MANAGE 'THE BIG SCREW UP'

*You have messed up and it's a do-or-die meeting. What to do?*

The CEO uses brevity to manage the big screw up.

Here is a hypothetical[2] scenario. Imagine you have messed up. The board of directors has summoned you tomorrow. Either you get kicked out, or you stay. It's do-or-die[3] *What's your Houdini plan?* The longer you stay in the room with the directors, greater the chances of putting your foot in your mouth[4]. A no-trust vote means you are out the door. Just like that.

Here is the brevity script to manage the meeting

TAKE THE FLOOR with confidence and composure. Acknowledge the screw up happened.

DESCRIBE THE SCREW UP. Mention initial expectations and things that went wrong.

DESCRIBE HOW THE SCREW UP COULD HAVE BEEN AVOIDED. Be ruthlessly honest.

DESCRIBE HOW YOU CONTRIBUTED TO THE SCREW UP. If you don't do this now, the next step won't stick.

PRESENT THE SOLUTION. There is always a solution.

STATE THAT ONLY YOU CAN CLEAN THE MESS, because you contributed to it.

OFFER A POUND OF FLESH[5] to show you mean what you say. In modern use, offering a pound of flesh means foregoing or giving away something precious to appease an injured party. This could mean foregoing privileges, perks, or remuneration for a specified period.

OUTLINE THE WAY FORWARD and wrap up the meeting.


## THE BREVITY SCRIPT — WHY IT WORKS

The brevity script disarms a hostile audience. The board of directors may have expected denial and airbrushing of facts. You said it quick, no beating around the bush. The brutally honest analysis of circumstances shifts the situation from pinning blame to problem solving. It creates a platform for constructive discussion.

Bringing in someone to clean up is not as easy as it sounds. No one wants to wash someone else's dirty laundry. You offered to clean up the mess.

You showed that you have no intention to resign. Retaining you saves company time and effort. Not keeping you could worsen a volatile situation. The options of shuffling members into new roles, or hiring from outside presents risks. There could be panic within the company, gossip that leaks out, and more. The board of directors want to leave the room with a sense of accomplishment. You give them that sense of accomplishment in a neat package.

---

*Up next* ☛ *CEO Habits — Clarity of Thought and Speech*

Clarity of thought and speech secures stakeholder buy-in.

# CHAPTER 5
# CLARITY OF THOUGHT AND SPEECH

# CEO HABITS
# CLARITY
# OF THOUGHT AND SPEECH

Quick question. If your thoughts are not clear, would your speech be clear?

When a manager, newbie or intern offers a long-winded, convoluted rationale for an action or decision, I do not see a clear thinker with sloppy speech. I see a sloppy thinker.

Leaders seek to influence. Clarity drives influence. Without clarity, the message does not reach the audience.

The CEO knows that clarity of thought and speech is a magnet that draws the audience in. When he speaks, people listen. Stakeholders buy in because the message hits home.

## HOW TO DEVELOP CLARITY OF THOUGHT AND SPEECH?

The starting point is honesty with the self, figuring out how things work and practicing zero level observation.

**HONESTY WITH THE SELF** Admit what you know and don't know.

Take, for example, your resume. It has words that describe your competencies. Strategist, proactive, team player, problem solver, creative thinker. Pick one and explain to a five-year-old what it means. If you can do this, you have clarity. If you can't, then it's *!@# sent to the recruiter.

Be honest with the self, so that clarity has space to grow.

**FIGURING OUT HOW THINGS WORK** Nothing beats actual knowledge. Figure out how things work.

Do you have a prized possession? A painting, artifact or souvenir? Google (or Yahoo or Bing) the processes that shaped it and allowed it to reach you. Narrate this journey to yourself in the mirror. Communicate the awesomeness of the process.

When you flex mental muscles, thoughts are clear. Clear speech follows.

**ZERO LEVEL OBSERVATION** is a hack for developing clarity of thought.

Take a seat in a park, mall or beach. Observe people going about their day. Let your eyes drift, or zoom in to something — it does not matter. The brain uses this time to rearrange thoughts and build heart-mind pathways. You may have heard, *"I need to clear my mind, I am going out for fresh air."* There is a gentle shake up that imparts clarity, and the brain knows how to do it.

---

The CEO does what it takes to develop clarity of thought and speech. It becomes a habit, trait, and an inseparable part of the persona. Reflect on the statement below.

> *Life offers few guarantees. But if you*
> *structure your thoughts and words well,*
> *that slight advantage is usually all you*
> *need to be ahead of the crowd — from*
> *GR8 Leaders Blog[1]*

## WHAT IF YOU NEED CLARITY OF THOUGHT AND SPEECH IN A HURRY?

Is it possible to fake-it-till-you-make-it?

Use the Here-There-Do[2] sequence to 'fake it'. It can be applied to scenarios such as stakeholder meetings for international cooperation, process improvement, budget allocation.

*Here-There-Do. The hack to appear intelligent and in control*

The Here-There-Do approach is simple. Present your idea or solution in the following sequence — we are here, we want to be there, this is what we do to get there. Arrange the slides in this sequence if you plan to use a slide deck.

The Here-There-Do approach forces clarity into the message and makes you appear smart.

The incorrect way of fake-it is 'wing-it[3]'. This means you start speaking and figure out the response along the way. We learn winging it at school. Traditional schooling rewards students who are quick to answer; they are perceived as engaged and attentive.

## MEDICAL CONDITIONS THAT MESS UP CLARITY OF THOUGHT AND SPEECH

DYSGRAPHIA[4] Trouble converting thoughts into writing.

EXPRESSIVE LANGUAGE DISORDER[5] Trouble converting thoughts into speech and writing.

RECEPTIVE LANGUAGE DISORDER[6] The person misinterprets instructions, ignores someone who is speaking to them, and does not recognize a joke — taking it as truth or fact.

## STRENGTH OF CHARACTER

Here is a quote that connects strength of character to clarity of thought and speech.

> *His clarity of thought, penetrating analyses*
> *and independence of spirit made him*
> *appear a strong character —*
> Anonymous, Cambridge
> Dictionary[7]

How is strength of character connected to clarity of thought and speech?

Strength of character is built upon courage and truth. Courage and truth dispel fear. One expresses with clarity when there is no fear.

*Up next* 👉 *CEO Habits — Learning by Observation*

Learning by observation is an efficient way to gather information.

# CHAPTER 6
# LEARNING BY OBSERVATION

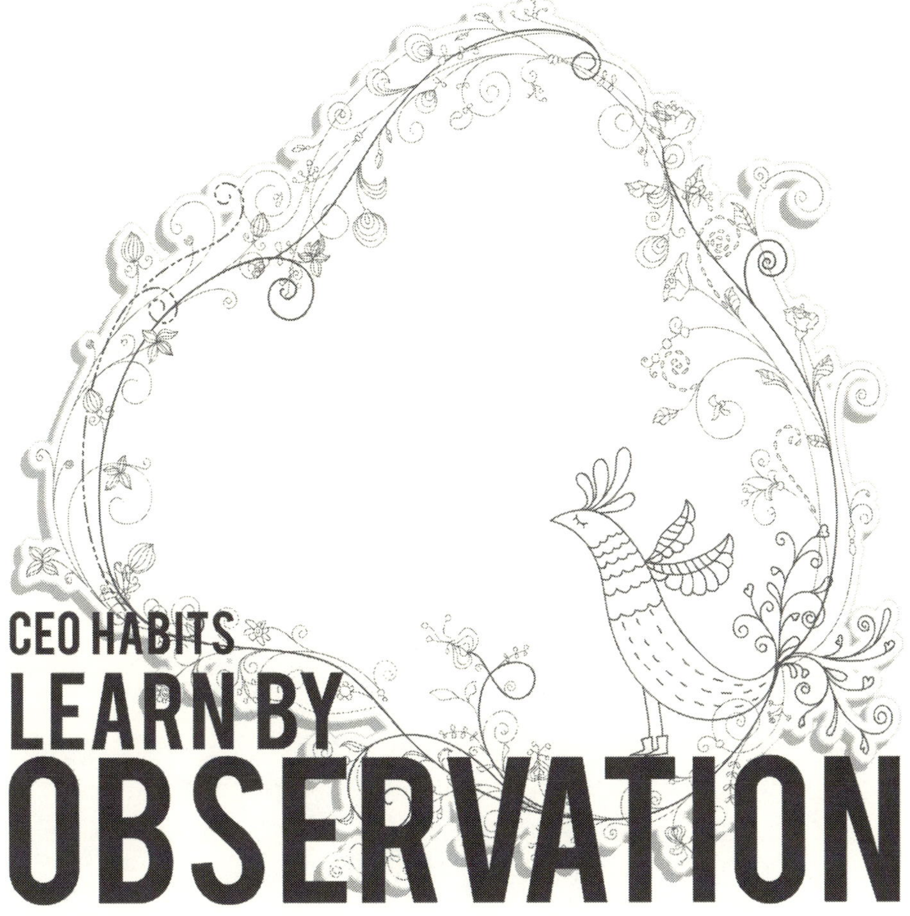



Few people observe. The CEO makes it a habit.

## WHAT DOES THE CEO OBSERVE?

The CEO observes herself and the elements[1] of her environment.

You: *Why would the CEO do that?*

Me: *Because, duh, that's the only way to know what's going on within the self and surrounding space.*

## FEW PEOPLE OBSERVE

Observation is the highest application of human intelligence. It is intense, performed concurrently[2] to another activity — for example, speaking, listening, having a meal — and must be processed to derive meaningful conclusions.

You: *Sounds deep…*

Me: *Yeah, there's more deep stuff here*  👇

- Observation produces raw data[3] — *this happened, that happened.* The stuff is not useful unless converted to meaningful conclusions.
- You must pick up the right data and draw the right conclusions. This requires a cognitive framework[4] for thought.
- The common impediments[5] to observation are confirmation bias[6], halo effect[7], and cognitive dissonance[8]. The umbrella term for these impediments is 'cognitive bias'. Cognitive bias causes you to draw incorrect conclusions from observations. The book 'Sensation & Perception'[9] is a primer to stuff that corrupts observation.

*"Hey, why can't I learn by making mistakes? I love making mistakes."*

You: *I thought one learns by doing, making mistakes, and failing. How does learning by observation fit in?*

Me: *Learning by doing, making mistakes and failing is useful to master skills, strategy, and complex tasks. Learning by observation is useful to gain advantage for yourself and the organization during workplace interaction. When you observe to learn, you know what's going on and you can plan your actions for greater impact.*

## OBSERVATIONS ON OBSERVATION

THE ABILITY TO OBSERVE diminishes in familiar surroundings. Many road accidents are reported close to the destination, near the home or place of work.

IN THE ANIMAL WORLD, prey and predators are biologically engineered to observe differently.

A myth associated with observation is that it is a natural human activity. This is incorrect. The natural disposition is to have tunnel vision. Fear and urgency trigger tunnel vision, impeding observation.

Multi-modal and visual learners use observation as primary means of learning, even for complex skills and tasks. Take the VARK[10] Modalities test to know your learning preferences.

Individuals with self-awareness are natural observers. Self-awareness is called intra-personal skill in personality assessment tests. The Multiple Intelligences[11] test gives you a score for intra-personal skill.

Egocentricity and self-awareness are inversely connected. Egocentricity means you place yourself at the center of the universe. Greater is the egocentricity, lesser is the self-awareness.

*"Me. Nothing else matters."*

# GETTING STARTED WITH LEARNING BY OBSERVATION

- IT IS OKAY for others to notice the observation activity. However, observation need not be in-your-face obviously. The duck paddles furiously underwater, but seems to glide on the surface. Similarly, the 'gaze' of observation is calm, friendly and attentive. Do you have a video of yourself at a meeting? Use it as a baseline to tweak your body language.
- INSPECT YOUR EYE-GLASSES Smaller eye frames compromise peripheral vision and lead to pronounced head movements. Consider wider eye frames.
- USE A NOTEPAD AND PEN as camouflage tools. Looking down to scribble a note provides a transition to discreetly shift your gaze from one subject to another.

---

THE BEST OF OBSERVERS think beyond themselves. The government employee observes for the nation. The nurse observes for the patient and healthcare institution. The civil defense front-liner observes for the citizen and the city. The sales person observes for the customer and the organization.

---

*Up next* ☛ *CEO Habits — Speed of Action*

Speed of follow-through keeps you top-of-mind with stakeholders.

# CHAPTER 7
# SPEED OF FOLLOW-THROUGH

# CEO HABITS
# SPEED
# OF FOLLOW THROUGH

Which is true? Speed is the enemy of quality. Speed is the hallmark of quality. Pick an answer.

You know the answer when you know what speed is not. Speed is not haste. Speed is the hallmark of quality.

The processing speed of your smartphone, gaming laptop and multimedia workstation drives performance. Speed is excellence on wheels.

At the workplace, we love the guy who gets stuff done quickly even when there is no deadline. Speed of follow-through is the CEO's tool to gain top-of-the-mind status.

Whether you compete with 200+ countries to host an event, or do good on the favor requested by a friend, speed builds equity. Make speed of follow-through your USP.

## SPEED OF FOLLOW-THROUGH ELICITS HEATED DEBATE

Speed of follow-through elicits heated debate amongst managers, newbies and interns.

The manager says, *"Company culture penalizes speed. Doing something immediately can make it seem an easy task."*

*"Speed of follow-through killed me."*

The newbie says, *"Colleagues warn me against delivering assignments quickly. They say people will route more work to you. You will die at the desk. And when you don't match the initial speed, it will be pointed out as a performance issue."*

The intern says, *"I don't know enough about the company to speed up. And it makes certain employees look bad. I want to build rapport, not foster rivalry."*

These are valid concerns. Your speed of follow-through must be matched by corresponding institutional muscles of speed. The litmus test of a great work culture is speed, and many fail the test.

However, none of these concerns stack up. Speed and agility are the competencies for uncertain times. In a VUCA[1] world, nations, economies, government, and companies must be agile[2]. Agility is delivered by humans[3], not entities. That means you.

CEO Dave Girouard[4] shares his tips for making speed fundamental to your company culture in the blog article[5] Speed as a Habit[6]. He says, *"There are decisions that deserve days of debate and analysis, but the vast majority aren't worth over 10 minutes"*.


## GETTING STARTED WITH SPEED OF FOLLOW-THROUGH

**MANIPULATIVE COLLEAGUES** will attempt to exploit your capacity for speed. Manage manipulative colleagues by creating a dependency for the proposed tasks.

Blogger and Style Advisor Antonio Centeno[7] says, *"When someone asks me to write about a complex product on my blog with an urgent timeline, I ask for a 100 — 200 word email that breaks down the product into bite-sized layman friendly information. I request it to be sent on an urgent timeline — the same day. If the email arrives, I get clear instructions. If not, then it means the product promotion is not important enough for them."*

A dependency helps you to confirm the urgency and authenticity of the proposed task. The tactic works best when the task is requested as a favor. Or when a team member won't provide a job brief.

## APPRAISE YOURSELF

**DON'T DEPEND ON THE ORGANIZATION** to appraise your speed of follow-through. Measure yourself against your own metrics. Build your own performance KPIs. The ones provided by your organization are not enough, sometimes wrong, often myopic. Measure yourself by the day, not month or quarter. These will become the habits that serve you across a lifetime.

*"Can't wait to be huge!"*

CEO Gary Vaynerchuk[8] says, *"So many people don't understand. In the day-to-day, they are slow. And in the macro, they want the business to be huge tomorrow. They are worrying about the years gone by, while wasting their days. If you are honest with yourself, I think a lot of you will find out that you really didn't work fast. 18, 17, 14, 12 I don't care about the numbers. I care about what you are doing in those hours. Speed. Bring it every day… in everything."*

**SAY NO** to assignments when you can and when you should.

**SPEED AND PATIENCE** work together. Speed at the execution level, patience at the global level. Extract the max from each second you put into work, but know that the business will not skyrocket next year. It will still take the same time. But the ROI on your efforts will be larger.

*Up next ☞ CEO Habits — Situational Awareness*

Situational awareness creates a negotiation advantage for the CEO.

# CHAPTER 8
# SITUATIONAL AWARENESS

T he master magician steps onto the stage. The audience believes *this time* they will figure out how he pulls off the sleight of hand.

A few minutes into the show and the audience gives up. They enjoy the show, clapping with glee and cheering the magician.

The magician controls the situational awareness of the audience to pull off stunts. What do they know about the human mind that we don't?

Authors Stephen L. Macknik and Susana Martinez-Conde are neuroscientists turned magicians. The book Sleights of Mind[1] shares the neuroscience of magic and reveals everyday deceptions. They say, *"Magic tricks work because humans have a hard-wired process of attention and awareness that is hackable. Magicians hack our brains, period.* **The same cognitive tricks are at work in advertising strategy, business negotiations and interpersonal relations.***"*

Speaker and magician Mac King shares an incident[2] that happened on stage. He was supposed to pull a live goldfish from his mouth and drop it into a glass of water. While the fish was in the mouth, it decided to swim down his throat. He turned around and vomited, throwing up bits of sandwich from lunch *and* the fish. He has extra fish, so he recovered and finished the trick. No one in the audience reacted to the glitch or asked him about it later. *"Everyone saw it. It's so weird. I don't know what's going on in people's minds."* Neuroscientists Stephen L. Macknik and Susana Martinez-Conde say, *"... the audience hardly ever notices. You believe you are aware of your surroundings. But* **at any given moment, you are blocking out 95% of all that is happening.** *The greatest magic show on earth is the one happening in your brain right now. An artist makes a flat canvas seem like a beautiful landscape, rich in depth. Magicians manipulate attention and cognition. Sleight of hand, pick-pocketing, mentalism and bamboozlement depend upon manipulating situational awareness."*

Not only humans are less aware, we enjoy tricks of illusion as works of art and mastery. This means situational awareness is not our default programming. It must be developed.

## SITUATIONAL AWARENESS TO SUSTAIN ADVANTAGE

The CEO develops situational awareness to sustain advantage during negotiations and stakeholder interaction. He trains his brain to pick up cues that amplify personal power, strategic advantage, and profitable future actions.

## THE WORD 'SITUATIONAL AWARENESS'

The word 'situational awareness' belongs to fields of study called *Decision-Making* and *Human Factors Psychology*. Situational awareness is a parameter of performance measurement and a driver of organizational excellence in air traffic control, cyber security, maritime surveillance, disaster response, tactical combat, bush craft survival.

## SITUATIONAL AWARENESS IN ACTION

*Didn't have situational awareness*

Lack of situational awareness is fatal if you are engaged in air combat, bush craft, or a sniper assignment. A tribal woman exercises situational awareness when she reads the forest for safety, opportunity, hazard, shift in circumstances. You do the same when driving.

Author Jason Hanson[3] says in the book 'Spy Secrets That Can Save Your Life'[4], *"People are often surprised when I tell them the most important thing I learned in the CIA is situational awareness. It's our knowledge of situational awareness that allows us to act before a crisis occurs. CIA officers receive the best possible training to ward off attack, escape restraints in seconds, and know what to do in a car chase — but it's situational awareness that's going to keep an officer alive."*

Cut to the corporate scenario. The CEO may be at a meeting, on a field visit, or at an event. S(he) is here to exploit opportunities and defuse threats as guardian of the organization and the community. The CEO 'reads the room' — what is happening, what has happened, what could happen.

Managers, newbies and interns who apply situational awareness are labeled 'street smart'. Take it as a compliment. Medical sales representatives (the guys with a big black bag and crisp suit waiting outside the doctor's office) arrive at the clinic ahead of the appointment time. They are here to gather intelligence, build situational awareness, establish rapport with clinic staff *and* pitch products to the physician. They observe the volume of patients lined up to see the physician. They observe the physician's rapport with clinic staff and other physicians. They note which reps meet with which physician. They chat with the pharmacist next door to learn about the physician's prescription preferences. Each day on the field yields information that steers the med rep's business decisions.

## DYNAMIC AND UNFAMILIAR ENVIRONMENTS

Situational awareness is compromised in dynamic and unfamiliar environments. You may experience

DATA OVERLOAD because your environment transforms at a rapid pace and you lose cognitive traction. Overcoming data overload is a central challenge for information dense environments, such as military operations, some process control systems, and real-time data analysis tasks[5].

ATTENTION TUNNELING because you stop scanning the environment to focus on something that holds your attention. Focusing on a single item without being disturbed by other stimuli is a part of information processing. However, there is a tradeoff between attention focus and the ability to process other events[6]. One cannot do both at the same time.

REQUISITE MEMORY TRAP where individuals are unable to capture vital information due to an overworked short term memory[7]. The short-term memory is full and cannot accommodate further inputs.

Manage dynamic and unfamiliar environments by chunking data and framing the environment. It is achieved through a preliminary visual scan and chunking information into categories — immediate attention and eventual attention, familiar and unfamiliar, relevant and irrelevant.

## READING PEOPLE

Reading people is a part of situational awareness.

Reading a person, group or audience means figuring out their current state of mind so you know what to do next. Spouses read each other naturally. At the workplace, bias, prejudice and laziness prevent us from reading people accurately.

## THE OBJECTIVE OF READING PEOPLE

The objective of reading people is to determine the authenticity of what they say and to uncover what they don't want to say. The bonus benefit of reading people is that you become conscious of how others read you.

To read criminals, spies and terrorists, interrogators develop mastery of body language. In business, the manager, newbie and intern who masters body language gains competitive and negotiation advantage, establishes rapport with customers quickly, mitigates hostility, and becomes a star salesperson.

Body language mastery is crucial to the effectiveness of the CEO's leadership. It drives the CEO's ability to manage change, build trust and foster collaboration.

## A WORD OF CAUTION

Body language must be interpreted as a cluster of behavioral cues within the context of culture, social norms, and personal baseline. An amateur approach to interpretation will incur embarrassment.

## BOOKS TO READ

Build body language mastery by standing on the shoulders of giants. Pick a couple of books from here or create your own reading list at the nearest library. These books should be in the company reading room. More books in this endnote[8].

**What Every BODY Is Saying[9] — An ex-FBI agent's guide to speed reading people.** By Joe Navarro with Marvin Karlins.

**The Body Language Advantage[10] — Maximize your personal and professional relationships with this ultimate photo guide to deciphering what others are secretly saying, in any situation.** By Lillian Glass.

**Body Language**[11] **— Learn how to read others and communicate with confidence.** By Elizabeth Kuhnke.

**The Silent Language Of Leaders**[12] **— How body language can help or hurt how you lead.** By Carol Kinsey Goman.

**Reading People**[13] **— How to understand people and predict their behavior, anytime, anyplace.** By Jo-Ellan Dimitrius and Mark Mazzarella.

**The Definitive Book of Body Language**[14] **— The hidden meaning behind people's gestures and expressions.** By Allan & Barbara Pease.

## GETTING STARTED WITH SITUATIONAL AWARENESS

You need to know

SITUATIONAL AWARENESS MEANS READING PEOPLE AND THE SURROUNDING SPACE. This is your interaction zone. It could be a stakeholder meeting, team huddle or technical training. Arrive early to gain situational intelligence. Being late whips up anxiety. Being on time gives you no advantage, that's when everyone else arrives.

SITUATIONAL AWARENESS MEANS USING WHAT YOU SEE TO BUILD A PICTURE OF WHAT'S GOING ON. When you are in the interaction zone, pay attention to activities and interaction not directly related to you. Don't default to glancing at the smartphone and texting while waiting or on a break.

**SITUATIONAL AWARENESS MEANS CONNECTING THE PICTURE OF WHAT'S GOING ON TO IMMEDIATE POSSIBILITIES.** The Universe brings you information, coincidences and serendipity to meet your goals. You are always in the right place at the right time. Make the connection between what you see and where it takes you.

**SITUATIONAL AWARENESS MEANS CONNECTING THE IMMEDIATE PICTURE TO DESIRED FUTURE EVENTS.** The circumstances of today hold the promise of tomorrow. Read the circumstances. You only know what you know. You won't know that you missed a chance meeting or vital piece of information when you weren't looking.

## AN EXAMPLE

Here's an example of lack of situational awareness (among other things) displayed by my team.

One of my business teams wanted to sell a clinical skills training model to the local college of medicine. The product was recently launched and the sales training was pending. All the same, the team was eager to pitch it and thought they could wing it. They shared product information with the faculty at the college. Faculty members were skeptical, but agreed to evaluate the device and requested a demonstration. On the appointed date, the business team set up the training model. Only a couple of faculty arrived on time and sat in silence. The business team was also silent because they had not rehearsed the pitch, and rapport was not yet established. Someone coaxed the rest of the faculty into the room and the demonstration began. Needless to say, it was not a customer-centric pitch. The faculty was polite and asked a few questions. They enquired whether they could keep the training model at the college for a week. The business team agreed, and the faculty filed out of the room. My boys read the circumstances as favorable, high-fived each other and reported that it was a successful demonstration. At the end of the week, the faculty had zero interaction with the training model. The team tried to leverage relationships and push the sale. The opportunity dragged on for months and eventually petered out.

Situational awareness could have highlighted the lack of engagement and natural outcome of the opportunity.

---

*Up next* ☛ *CEO Habits — Executive Presence*

Executive presence leads a team to glory and steers the company to safety in a crisis.

# CHAPTER 9
## EXECUTIVE PRESENCE

# CEO HABITS
# EXECUTIVE PRESENCE

Executive presence is the UI/UX[1] of You.

It is the invisible billboard that says you lead, influence and inspire. You command the room with ease without towering over others.

Few would land a top job, win a landmark deal, or develop a following without executive presence.

Executive presence is built around the perception of competence, likability and trustworthiness. S(he) is the wo(man) you think will lead the team to glory and steer the company to safety in a crisis.

## DAY-TO-DAY BENEFIT OF EXECUTIVE PRESENCE

Executive presence builds bridges quickly. The bridge may be connections, relationships or referrals. It overcomes barriers quickly. The barriers may be diversity, language, culture, or bidding on a turnkey project for the first time. It makes your team feel powerful and believe that anything is possible.

## BUSTING THE MYSTERY

The CEO knows that executive presence is a *blend* whose sum is greater than the parts. But one must refrain from labeling it a mystery, art, and such stuff. Executive presence has been decoded, taught and honed successfully.

## THE BUILDING BLOCKS OF EXECUTIVE PRESENCE

Executive presence is built upon these traits and core competencies

Confidence to make difficult decisions These are examples of difficult decisions — disclosure to shareholders of fraud within the company, announcing company-wide layoffs, shutting down parts of the business, implementing gender balance and no-discrimination policies, reviewing misuse of perks with an employee who is also a buddy, telling the top performing department that they are not putting in their best, letting a long-term employee go. These decisions place the organization at risk of losing trust and leverage. The CEO is a critical thinker who makes difficult decisions with confidence and clarity.

COMPOSURE IN A CRISIS Crises are a part of the lifecycle of the organization. The CEO learns composure and crisis management *before* wearing the CEO pin.

Author Sylvia Ann Hewlett[2] shares in the book, 'Executive Presence'[3], "Bob Dudley[4] has been at the epicenter of the industry's worst nightmares. During an interview, he said — I want people around me who can be clear-thinking and calm in a crisis. I don't believe I've ever been able to judge or trust a person unless I can see what they're like under fire."

INTEGRITY TO MAKE THE RIGHT DECISIONS Integrity is always a choice and often the best choice. The CEO can balance ethics and organizational interests during difficult decisions.

OWNING UP TO MISTAKES CEOs have publicly admitted mistakes and faced the flak. To everyone's surprise, it built credibility, trustworthiness and equity.

DECISIVENESS UNDER UNCERTAINTY Uncertainty can paralyze. Is it better to act when the picture clears? Or is it better to push the picture to clarity by doing *something*? Agile or pro-active, what's the way forward?

The CEO does not ride uncertainty through inaction. He reads the circumstances and crafts the outcomes that create value.

FEROCIOUS IN SAFEGUARDING STAKEHOLDER INTERESTS Stakeholders are customers, colleagues, company, nation and community. Organizational outcomes must be favorable across stakeholders. The earth and its ecosystem is also a stakeholder. Destroying natural habitat to build a tyre factory that spews noxious emissions does nothing for executive presence.

CONGENIALITY The CEO wears his dazzling competence lightly. He aims to inspire, not intimidate. The ancient advice to wise men is, "Be a tree. Stay rooted and keep the shade of your presence cool."

ELOQUENCE AND BREVITY When times are tough, the organization is a rocky boat with employees in panic mode. The CEO communicates the way forward. He restores clarity, direction, and hope. The CEO knows that without hope nothing matters.

Of course, one can only convey what is aligned with character. Author Christopher Witt says in the book, 'Real Leaders Don't Do Powerpoint'[5], "*You* are the message. The message listeners hear is shaped by who you are, what you've done and what you value."

CLOSING THE LOOP The CEO closes the loop on action, communication and deliverables. If you find that (s)he hasn't, evaluate whether (s)he really needs to be involved, whether you inadvertently crossed a boundary or didn't pull your own weight on it first.

These traits and core competencies support grooming, attire, diction and body language factors to build executive presence.

## EXCEPTIONS TO THE RULE

Mahatma Gandhi[6], Nelson Mandela[7], Steve Jobs[8], Nouman Ali Khan[9], BK Shivani[10], Vandana Shiva[11] are individuals who demonstrate(d) minimal focus on grooming and attire. Their executive presence is built on the strength of intrinsic traits and core competencies.

---

*Up next* ☛ *CEO Habits — Spotting The Black Swan*

Spotting the black swan shifts business outcomes in your favor.

# CHAPTER 10
# SPOTTING THE BLACK SWAN

# CEO HABITS
# SPOTTING THE BLACK SWAN

Swans are white. You don't think it's gonna happen — spotting a black swan.

Well, it happened. The black swan was spotted in the seventeenth century. And everything we knew about swans came under review. Black swans have always existed. But for centuries, we didn't have a clue.

Author Nassim Nicholas Taleb[1] says in the book 'The Black Swan'[2], "Swans are white. Empirical evidence extending across millennia confirmed this. The sighting of the first black swan illustrated the fragility of our knowledge. One observation invalidated the sightings of millions of white swans. All you need is one black bird! The black swan is an outlier, it lies outside the realm of regular expectations, because nothing in the past pointed to its possibility. The black swan has extreme impact; textbooks must be re-written, and zoological classification overhauled. Despite its outlier status, humans concoct explanations for the black swan's occurrence, deeming it explainable and predictable.

The combination of low predictability and large impact makes the black swan intriguing for social scientists."

The term Black Swan is used to illustrate events in business, economics and disaster response. A black swan event is a highly improbable, highly consequential event that occurs without warning and turns everything upside down — a tsunami, economic crash, a shootout at school. It happens suddenly and changes the way we do things.

We place trust in 'the system' to prevent, or at least forecast and control, mega shocks. But a black swan event overrides the system. Does it really? In hindsight, the warning signs are visible. But no one was looking or connecting the dots.

## BLACK SWANS IN NEGOTIATIONS

Ex-FBI Agent, Hostage Negotiator and Author Chris Voss describes the Black Swan in the book 'Never Split The Difference'. He says, "Black Swans are hidden and unexpected pieces of information whose unearthing has game-changing effects on a negotiation dynamic. Negotiation breakthroughs — when the game shifts unalterably in your favor — are created by those who can identify and utilize Black Swans."

## THE SUCKER'S TRAP

> The sucker's trap — you focus on what you know and what others don't know, rather than the reverse. *Nassim Nicholas Taleb* ❇ *The Bed of Procrustes*

Chris Voss[3] says, "There is the visible negotiation and then the things hidden under the surface — the secret negotiation space wherein the Black Swans dwell."

The CEO knows that the Black Swan is a piece of the puzzle not with her in a negotiation, yet. (S)he does not predict negotiation outcomes based on past experience. She avoids the sucker's trap.

## THE UNKNOWN UNKNOWNS

In a negotiation, there are things we know. These are ***known-knowns***. There are things we know that we don't know. We call these gaps. These are ***known-unknowns***. There are things outside the horizon of our knowledge, frame of reference and experience. These are ***unknown-unknowns*** — the Black Swans. Every negotiation has more than one Black Swan.

## BLACK SWANS IN BUSINESS NEGOTIATIONS

In business negotiations, Black Swans are uncovered through questions and active listening. Other than insider information, of course; which is beyond the scope of the book.

The primary challenge in using questions to reveal Black Swans is that you may not know which questions to ask. The other challenge is you will not hear everything the first time. What do you do?

A tactic used by negotiators — rephrase a question. It uncovers new information, highlights discrepancy or consistency, and advances the negotiation. Use backup listeners whose job is to listen and observe. They will pick up the things you miss. Keep an open mind to see and hear things that can produce negotiation breakthroughs. Tune into information and strategic advantage served up by the moment. Do not overvalue past negotiation experience.

One of the things to determine in a sales negotiation is whether the other side's vision of the future involves them staying involved with the outcomes of the decision. If your counterpart is planning to leave the job, he may *want* to sabotage a great deal that benefits the current employer. This knowledge is your black swan.

Black swans aren't always 'important and secret' information. It may be something that has least significance to your counterpart. It may be a piece of information whose value they do not understand.

A broker for a prime piece of property innocently revealed that the seller has other real estate assets that are not doing well. This was a black swan for the buyer. He figured the seller needed the money to support those assets. It helped him close quickly at a price much lower than what he had targeted.

A black swan could be the other side's worldview. Determine the other side's worldview and speak the language that is consistent with it. Deals have been closed swiftly because the counterpart felt understood.

People have rules for life. When you know your counterpart's rules for life, you can use them to shift the odds in your favor. For example, it is common to buy cars and real estate with cash in the Middle East. This is because of culture and a theological belief that interest-based financial instruments are the root of economic evil. This is a black swan for the overseas property developer. If he designs the pitch around a great mortgage plan, the pitch will fail because it breaks the prospect's rules for life. People seldom break their own rules for life. These black swans can stall a negotiation or take you to a close.

Another black swan is the person or ideology that your negotiation counterpart respects as 'the authority'. This could be a business ideology, a sense of stewardship[4], personal rules of honor, faith in their own diligent research, or a specific person such as a KOL[5]. Your job is to uncover who is the authority for the other side. That's your black swan. Remember there is only one authority that people listen to — the one they have created themselves. You win when the other side thinks your proposal is aligned with the authority.

## FEAR OF BLACK SWANS

It is human nature to fear the unknown. Go past the fear. Uncover black swans to create an enviable track record of negotiation wins. Build negotiation muscles with this reading list

**Never Split The Difference[6] — Negotiating as if your life depended on it.** By Chris Voss with Tahl Raz

**Negotiation Genius[7] — How to overcome obstacles and achieve brilliant results at the bargaining table and beyond.** By Deepak Malhotra and Max H. Bazerman.

**Getting (More Of) What You Want[8] — How the secrets of economics and psychology can help you negotiate anything, in business and life.** By Margaret A. Neale and Thomas Z. Lys

**Getting To Yes[9] — Negotiating agreement without giving in**. By Roger Fisher, William Try and Bruce Patton.

**Getting Past No[10] — Negotiating in difficult situations.** By William Try.

---

*Up next ☛ CEO Habits — Attention To Detail*

Attention to detail is the CEO's tool to manage complexity.

# CHAPTER 11
# ATTENTION TO DETAIL

Here is a trick question. Attention to detail means zeroing in, sharp focus. True or false.

The correct answer is False.

## STOP THINKING AND PAY ATTENTION

Joseph Cardillo[1] shares the teachings of Swordsman, Philosopher and Strategist Miyamoto Musashi[2] in the book 'Can I Have Your Attention — How to think fast, find your focus and sharpen your concentration'. He says[3], "*My sensei[4] asked me to stop thinking and just pay attention. It confused me. I thought I was paying attention.*"

Musashi teaches that, to the swordsman, deterioration of attention means death. When a swordsman stands against an opponent, he is not to *think* about his enemy, himself, or the movement of swords. He must think of *nothing* and allow what is in the unconscious to surface and take over. That is attention. The Japanese call it *mushin (無心* no mind)[5]. According to the ancient masters, *mushin* is operating when your mind's attention moves from one activity to another, without the interference of thought. It is analogous to flow experienced by artists immersed in a creative process[6]. Your mind flows like a stream of hyper-alert water, filling every space in your environment. *Mushin* is a coveted state of mind all martial artists strive to reach.

Seems opposed to logic, doesn't it? Attention needs absence of thought and intention. It is logical when you realize that the complexity of offensive-defensive moves, anticipating the enemy's moves, and protecting the self in real-time cannot be handled through thought.

## DEPICTION OF MUSHIN IN MOVIES

The Hollywood movie 'The Last Samurai'[7] has a scene where Tom Cruise is captured by the samurai and begins to admire his captors. He becomes a disciple and learns the way of samurai. In a scene that involves mushin, Tom Cruise is learning how to wield a sword. He has been defeated in sparring yet again. His opponent tries to explain, *"Please forgive, you have too many mind. You have mind sword, mind people watch, mind enemy. Too many mind. Must have no mind."*

Throughout the movie, Tom Cruise's swordsmanship improves when his understanding of mushin settles in. He finally defeats his sparring partner.

## ATTENTION TO DETAIL AT THE WORKPLACE

'Attention to detail' and 'attention' (mushin) are related but not the same.

Coach and Author Chris Denny[8] explains attention to detail in the video, 'The 3 Types Of Attention To Detail'[9]. He advises, *"Whether you are an individual who wants to reduce errors or want to foster a culture of attention to detail across the organization, identify where your problems lie and where you want the improvements to come from."*

The three types of attention to detail are contrastive, analytical and additive.

Contrastive attention to detail fixes right or wrong issues — spelling errors, forgetting to mention something on product packaging, posting the wrong URL on social media.

Analytical attention to detail steers the outcomes of complex interactions — business negotiations, political conflict, criminal trials, human rights review, diplomatic discussions, bid qualification meetings. In these scenarios, you have limited information in certain areas, there is a lot happening in the room, and you must look for clues to pull out a solution.

Additive attention to detail enhances the outcomes of creative and technical tasks — new product development, UI/UX of a device, ambience of a restaurant.

Chris Denny shares, *"Additive attention to detail is about making a product, service or experience better, or amazing. This is what you think of, when you go to a restaurant and end up saying — it's the attention to detail that sets them apart. It's because there is someone with additive attention to detail on the team who understands that details matter, that certain things need to be in place, or not be there, for visitors to have an exceptional experience.*

*Steve Jobs was renowned for this kind of thing. He had so much additive attention to detail that it almost fell into the contrastive category.*

*It is important to know the types of attention to detail, because if you are trying to improve as an individual or organization, you know where to focus."*

CEO and Founder of Virgin, Richard Branson says, *"When making experiences, attention to detail matters."* This is a reference to additive attention to detail.

## THE CONNECTION BETWEEN MUSHIN AND ANALYTICAL ATTENTION TO DETAIL

Mastering mushin helps develop analytical attention to detail. It enhances your ability to toggle through focus-or-execute settings, manage information overload, and trains your mind to avoid being hooked by a single point of information. It keeps you calm up to the point of action.

The CEO builds analytical attention to detail into a habit. During a negotiation, dispute, discussion, or meeting, he manages data overload and scans the environment for clues that matter. He knows what good looks like and steers outcomes in that direction. Analytical attention to detail requires intense data crunching in real-time. The mental activity must be discreet and invisible to others. Hence, it has to be a *habit*.

## TRICKS OF THE BRAIN

*Hmmm… interesting!*

You spot a scratch on your sparkling new dream car, even though you don't actively look for it. But you fail to spot dust and grease on the laptop, sometimes for days. What's going on, you ask (or at least you should). The brain likes to conserve resources. Like a lazy loading web page, the brain exerts effort only when it thinks it necessary.

The brain uses previous learning to fill in missing information. Show the brain a paragraph with spelling errors and missing letters; the brain glosses over the errors and still reads it correctly.

The brain has its own opinion on what is important and what isn't. In the fun experiment Change Blindness[10], many students failed to notice that the person offering cupcakes was replaced. The brain is like, *"Do you think I care if the person is same or not?"* Watch it here[11].

Author and Professor at The Harvard Business School, Max H. Bazerman[12] shares an experiment in the book 'The Power Of Noticing — What the best leaders see'[13], *"Mahzarin Banaji[14] played a video by psychologist Ulric Neisser[15]. We were supposed to count the number of passes a team had made. Many got it wrong. I was pleased to be one of the few that got it correct. Then, Mahzarin asked about the woman with an open umbrella in the video. I hadn't noticed the woman with an open umbrella. She replayed the clip and there it was — the woman walking across the floor with an open umbrella in the most obvious manner. I hadn't noticed because I was busy counting passes. When I show this video in classrooms, my students, like me, focus on counting and generally miss this very obvious information in their visual world. Years after I saw the video for the first time, I remain obsessed by my failure to see the woman with the umbrella, and this obsession has organized my research and teaching over the past decade.*" Watch a similar version of this experiment The Monkey Business Illusion[16]

These examples indicate that attention to detail is not natural. The brain must be trained, or re-trained to notice stuff that you deem relevant.

Since the brain behaves like a frenemy[17], one is tempted to confront it. "*Look buddy, you ain't cutting it right. We got room for improvement and I need your cooperation.*"

Well, actually it's you who gives the brain a hard time. One way you do it is by thinking when you should pay attention.

## FOOD FOR THOUGHT

✪ Joseph Cardillo[18] speaks about the gaze of attention demonstrated by his sensei, "*His eyes were wide and deep like a cat's; they seemed like mirrors—completely attentive, yet unthinking. This is what many refer to as the martial arts stare. My job was to journey into those mirrors and learn something about paying attention.*"

✪ Attention to detail is a process, not an ingredient in the excellence mix. Web developer and technology writer, Marco Arment[19] says, "*Attention to detail is never (and can't be) added later. It is a development philosophy, methodology, and culture."*

---

*Up next ☛ CEO Habits — Relationships For Life*

Relationships-for-life are the CEO's legacy.

# CHAPTER 12
# RELATIONSHIPS FOR LIFE

## CEO HABITS

# RELATIONSHIPS FOR LIFE

Relationships-for-profit don't last. The CEO nurtures *relationships-for-life*. It leads to organizational stability, consistent revenue, and business growth.

So what's the smooth-as-chocolate formula to relationships-for-life?

It starts with a mirror, my friend.

Look in the mirror. Are you the person with whom someone may *wish* to have a relationship-for-life? Do you have *ongoing* relationships-for-life in personal and professional life? Does your organization have a relationships-for-life *culture*?

## A RELATIONSHIP-FOR-LIFE STARTS *BEFORE* YOU HAVE MET THE STAKEHOLDER

Relationships-for-life are built when the business is *designed* to meet the stakeholder on *their* terms, when their feedback is used to build a *better, easier world* for them. Relationships-for-life are not built through opt-in subscriptions, targeted content or personalized mail. These are front-end tactics for short-term, conditional engagement controlled by the organization, not the stakeholder.

## THE ETHICS THAT GOVERN RELATIONSHIPS-FOR-LIFE

The term relationships-for-life means looking out for stakeholder interests, keeping communication lines open and meeting stakeholders *more* than halfway.

THE B2B CUSTOMER may ask you to source an inferior product with the lowest price. You do not give it to them. They need a product that delights *their* customers. Educate them and offer a portfolio of great stuff.

THE B2C CUSTOMER demands ROI[1] and a great price. Work through supply chain and vendors to bring down costs and improve functional design. Give the customer ways to reach you. Do not leave prospects stranded after a product promotion campaign on social media. It is common to see social media queries that remain unanswered, *"Where can I buy it? What does it cost?"* Invest in solutions that allow social media conversations from a single dashboard.

LOCAL SUPPLIERS are firms that provide services like business card printing, pantry supplies delivery, house-keeping, travel reservations, etc for your organization. The supplier has invested time in winning your business and trust. Do not drop him to save dollars on the next job or purchase. Competing suppliers may offer discounts. *"How much do you pay the current supplier? I can get the job done at a 10% lower cost."* The loss-leader tactic is a toxic loop that harms the industry and economy of the nation.

## RELATIONSHIPS-FOR-LIFE IS NOT ONLY FOR THE ENTERPRISE

Nations and governments invest in relationships-for-life to curb corruption and foster trust.

The United Arab Emirates (UAE) is an example of bold governance and relationships-for-life ethos[2] set by Sheikh Mohammed Bin Rashid Al Maktoum[3].

A BIT OF BACKGROUND Only 20% of UAE's residents are native citizens. The United Nations[4] ranks UAE among countries with the highest percent of immigrants. 80% of UAE's residents are immigrants[5] from over 200 countries,

The country is an autocracy — it has rulers, not elected heads of state. From 2006 to 2020, Sheikh Mohammed has sought to transform the Arab mindset. Generations of Arabs have lived in luxury on state funding in the past. Lethargy and a laid-back lifestyle were barriers to productivity. He dismantled the barriers through conditional state funding. He introduced transparency, accountability, and speed into governance. He demanded that residents be treated as customers and government departments function as an enterprise with customer excellence KPIs. For this reason, Sheikh Mohammed is referred to as The Sheikh CEO[6].

The government departments were accustomed to serving visitors on *their* terms — their timings, their procedure, their timeline. They didn't want to change. How does one convince government departments to function like an enterprise, create KPIs, and meet them? By enforcing personal accountability of departmental heads to the public.

In 2016, Sheikh Mohammed walked into government offices with a videographer filming live[7]. It was 8 am and several employees were not in their seats. He posted the video on social media. In the same week, he initiated the retirement of nine senior officials. It was a message that departmental heads have personal accountability to the people. *"He certainly wanted to send a message. Timeliness starts at the top and we won't go after employees when their bosses aren't there*[8]," Mona Al-Marri, director-general of the government of Dubai Media Office told Bloomberg. "*The changes infuse new blood, provide opportunities for promising young leaders and implement standards aligned with the highest quality of service across departments and bodies.*"

An annual ritual, on the lines of Wooden Spoon[9], is to announce the worst performing government departments[10][11][12] in a live telecast. As the announcements begin, the camera zooms to the face of the department head. It is a message that s(he) is personally accountable to the people.

Sheikh Mohammed holds himself equally accountable. He tweets and posts updates in real-time. Several mechanisms allow residents to share an idea, grievance or thought. Dubai Cares[13] was born when a lady walked in with a sheet outlining the idea[14].

In 2013, Sheikh Mohammed announced the transition from e-government to m-government on social media. He said, "*I want the government to operate round-the-clock and be a one-stop shop; where everything can be done easily using a smartphone. I promise those who will not enable this transformation within a year will be given a farewell party.*"[15]

The 2020 Global Law and Order Report by global analytics firm Gallup ranked UAE in the top ten countries worldwide for security and personal safety.[16] Gallup's annual *Global Law and Order* report allows world leaders to compare each country's progress towards the United Nations' goal of a peaceful and secure world.[17]

The 2021 Best Cities Report ranked Abu Dhabi and Dubai among the top 15 cities in the world.[18] Bloomberg[19] calls this report "the most comprehensive study of its kind; it identifies cities that are most desirable for locals, visitors, and businesspeople alike, rather than simply looking at livability or tourism appeal."[20]

Author Yasar Jarrar[21], former Director of Strategy at The Executive Office of Sheikh Mohammed Bin Rashid Al Maktoum shares in the book, 'The Sheikh CEO[22] — Lessons in leadership', "*The Edelman Trust Barometer[23] ranks UAE among the top 5 most trusted governments globally. The nation has a development model where the government and people work together as one. The government trusts the people and the people trust the government*".

Sheikh Mohammed's relationship with the residents of the UAE is a relationship-for-life. It was a one-way relationship when he initiated it. The reciprocal trust and engagement of the residents has transformed it into a two-way relationship.


## BUILDING RELATIONSHIP MUSCLES

To get started with relationships-for-life, you need relationship muscles.

❤ STRENGTHEN THE PRIMARY RELATIONSHIPS THAT MATTER — your relationship with the earth and the economy. Ditch the plastic. Buy something organic once a month. Send ripples down the supply chain. Motivate the earth-destroying capitalist to focus on recyclable packaging and organic produce.

❤ A RELATIONSHIP-FOR-LIFE IS ONE-WAY IN THE BEGINNING The other side does not owe you a relationship. For example, my companies liaise with multiple vendors across projects and global markets. A vendor declined to allocate a marketing budget for a 'low priority' market. As a distribution partner, I chose to absorb the cost and demonstrated the ROI. It transformed the relationship (and a marketing budget was allocated for the following year). The lesson is that you do not drop the ball early into the relationship.

❤ DREAM FOR STUFF LARGER THAN YOURSELF My dream is to work with medical technology vendors who have limited funds and expertise for selling overseas. These vendors build products that improve quality of life for children, elderly, and those receiving end-of-life care. I find these vendors online or at trade-shows, and am like, *"Man! This stuff must be available to everyone in the world who needs it."* I have a relationship with these vendors and the future beneficiaries of the solutions; even though I haven't met them yet. In my mind, the relationship is on.

❤ THE EMPLOYER — EMPLOYEE RELATIONSHIP The employee is a person. Umm, no. The employee is a bunch of thoughts that shift and evolve. You, the employer, are the peg that grounds the employee's thoughts and channels them towards good business practices. Your relationship with the employee must move beyond the transactional. When this happens, the culture that fosters relationships-for-life is established.

## AN EXTREME EXAMPLE

In 1940, a nexus of geographically concentrated evil arose, denser and darker than anything the world had ever seen. Over four years, more than 1.3 million people would be systematically sorted, enslaved, tortured, and murdered. And no one would do anything to stop it. This is the story of Captain Witold Pilecki[24] and Auschwitz[25].

Author Mark Manson shares in the book 'Everything is F*cked — A Book about Hope'[26], *"Auschwitz was a huge blind spot to the outside world. No one had an idea what was going on there and little chance of finding out.*

*Witold Pilecki decided to sneak into Auschwitz. Initially, it was a rescue mission — he would get himself arrested, coordinate a mutiny and get everyone out.*

*It was a mission so suicidal that his superiors thought he was crazy and told him as much.*

*Pilecki's commanders eventually relented. One evening, at a routine checkpoint, Pilecki let himself be arrested for violating curfew. And soon, he was on his way to Auschwitz, the only man known ever to have voluntarily entered a Nazi concentration camp.*

*Once he got there, he saw that the reality of Auschwitz was far worse than anyone had suspected. Prisoners were routinely shot in roll call lineups for transgressions as minor as fidgeting or not standing up straight. The manual labor was grueling and endless. Men were literally worked to death, often performing tasks that were useless or meant nothing.*

*The first month Pilecki was there, one-third of the men in his barracks died of exhaustion or pneumonia or were shot. Regardless, in a few months, Pilecki had still somehow set up an espionage operation."*

Pilecki created an intelligence network by embedding messages in laundry baskets, built a transistor radio out of spare parts and stolen batteries, and successfully transmitted plans for an attack on the prison camp to the outside world. He created smuggling rings to bring in food, medicine, and clothing for prisoners, saving countless lives and delivering hope.

Author Mark Manson wonders aloud, *"What did this world do to deserve Witold Pilecki?"*

Over the course of two years, Pilecki built a resistance unit within Auschwitz. He believed he could stoke a prison break and free everyone with help and coordination from the outside. He sent his plans and reports to the outside world. For months, he waited. For months, he survived. The outside world did not respond.

Then came more prisoners. arriving by the tens of thousands. They were filed mechanically into "shower" barracks, gassed, and their bodies burned.

Pilecki's reports to the outside became frantic. He said if you can't liberate the camp, then at least bomb it, at least destroy the gas chambers. The outside world concluded he was exaggerating. In the farthest reaches of their minds, oppressive activity of this scale was not possible. Talk about cognitive dissonance. His intelligence was forwarded through the various resistance groups around the world. They, too, figured Pilecki had to be exaggerating.

In 1943, nearly three years later, Pilecki realized that his plans of a mutiny and prison break would never happen. It was time to escape, and he did.

He led many more missions, each more unbelievable than the earlier. Despite witnessing and enduring years of war, torture, death and genocide, Pilecki never lost belief in being a force of good in the world.

Author Mark Manson says, *"This is a story of being f*cked on a scale that today, with the comfort of our free wifi and oversize snuggie blankets, you and I can hardly imagine. When we zoom out and get perspective, we realize that while heroes like Pilecki save the world, we swat at gnats and complain that the AC isn't high enough. Such stories make us say — What have I done lately? If this is not the most amazing story you've ever heard, then I want some of what you're having."*

Captain Witold Pilecki had a one-way relationship-for-life with the people whose lives he saved.

## PILECKI AND YOU

You aren't Pilecki, and you need not be. In business, it is far easier. Most of your one-way relationships will transform into mutually rewarding relationships.

You lead a privileged life that you did nothing to deserve. Let gratitude seep in. Then move your butt and go build that relationship-for-life.

***

*Up next* 👉 *The 12th Non-Habit*

Could you carry a message to Garcia?

# PART II

# CHAPTER 13
# THE 12TH NON-HABIT
## DON'T JUST DO AS I TELL YOU

THE 12TH NON-HABIT

# DON'T JUST DO AS I TELL YOU

"*Something is brewing on this project. Find out what's going on.*"

How would you interpret this? The instruction is to find out what's going on, nothing more.

The *unspoken* message is to do what is necessary within your role and opportunity, loop in everybody and keep going till the matter concludes.

This seems obvious, but employees thrive on instructions. They fail to develop the aptitude that minimizes a need for micro-instructions.

It is good practice to have micro-instructions, a precise brief or 'everything in writing' for technical tasks. However, it does not work at the strategic level, because of the uncertainty within circumstances.

Bob Nelson, author of the book 'Please don't just do what I tell you! Do what needs to be done' says, "I know of no company today that can survive with employees doing only what they are told to do. You never need permission to do great work."

## CARRY A MESSAGE TO GARCIA

Have you heard the phrase "carry a message to Garcia"?

It means independently fulfilling a task that has many challenges and no easy answers. The phrase originates from an essay penned in the nineteenth century.

*A Message to Garcia*[1] was written by Elbert Hubbard[2] in 1899. The essay refers to a daring escapade performed by 1st Lt. Andrew S. Rowan[3]. He carried a message from President William McKinley[4] to General Calixto García[5], prior to the Spanish-American War[6].

Elbert Hubbard compares Rowan to the average employee. Read on…

*A Message to Garcia, Elbert Hubbard, 1899*

*There is one man who stands out on the horizon of my memory.*

*When war broke out, it was necessary to communicate quickly with Garcia. He was somewhere in the mountains of Cuba — no one knew where. No mail or telegraph could reach him. The President must secure his cooperation, and quickly.*

*What to do!*

*Someone said to the President, "A fellow by the name of Rowan will find Garcia for you, if anybody can."*

*Rowan was sent for and given a letter to be delivered to Garcia. How "the fellow by name of Rowan" took the letter, sealed it up in an oil-skin pouch, strapped it over his heart, in four days landed by night off the coast of Cuba from an open boat, disappeared into the jungle, and in three weeks came out on the other side of the island, having traversed a hostile country on foot, and having delivered his letter to Garcia, are things I have no special desire now to tell in detail.*

*The point I wish to make is this: McKinley gave Rowan a letter to be delivered to Garcia; Rowan took the letter and did not ask, "Where is he at?"*

*By the Eternal! There is a man whose form should be cast in bronze and the statue placed in every college in the land!*

*No man who has endeavored to carry out an enterprise where many hands were needed, but has been well-nigh appalled at times by the imbecility of the average man — the inability or unwillingness to concentrate on a thing and do it.*

*Slipshod assistance, foolish inattention, dowdy indifference, and half-hearted work seem the rule; and no man succeeds, unless by hook or crook, or threat, he forces or bribes other men to assist him; or mayhap, God in His goodness performs a miracle, and sends him an Angel of Light for an assistant.*

*You, reader, put this matter to a test: You are sitting now in your office—six clerks are within your call. Summon anyone and make this request: "Please look in the encyclopedia and make a brief memorandum for me concerning the life of Corregio."*

*Will the clerk quietly say, "Yes, sir", and go do the task?*

*On your life, he will not. He will look at you out of a fishy eye and ask one or more of the following questions:*

*Who was he?*

*Which encyclopedia?*

*Where is the encyclopedia?*

*Was I hired for that?*

*Don't you mean Bismarck?*

*What's the matter with Charlie doing it?*

*Is he dead?*

*Is there any hurry?*

*Shan't I bring you the book and let you look it up yourself? What do you want to know for?*

*And I will lay you ten to one that after you have answered the questions, and explained how to find the information, and why you want it, the clerk will go off and get one of the other clerks to help him find Garcia — and then come back and tell you there is no such man. Of course I may lose my bet, but according to the Law of Average, I will not.*

*Now if you are wise, you will not bother to explain to your "assistant" that Corregio is indexed under the C's, not in the K's, but you will smile sweetly and say, "Never mind", and go look it up yourself. And this incapacity for independent action, this moral stupidity, this infirmity of the will, this unwillingness to cheerfully catch hold and lift, are the things that put pure socialism so far into the future. If men will not act for themselves, what will they do when the benefit of their effort is for all?*

*We have recently been hearing much maudlin sympathy expressed for the "down-trodden denizen of the sweatshop" and the "homeless wanderer searching for honest employment," and with it all often go many hard words for the men in power.*

*Nothing is said about the employer who grows old before his time in a vain attempt to get frowsy ne'er-do-wells to do intelligent work; and his long patient striving with "help" that does nothing but loaf when his back is turned. In every store and factory there is a constant weeding-out process going on. The employer is constantly sending away "help" that have shown their incapacity to further the interests of the business, and others are being taken on. No matter how good times are, this sorting continues, only if times are hard and work is scarce, this sorting is done finer — but out and forever out, the incompetent and unworthy go. It is the survival of the fittest. Self-interest prompts every employer to keep the best — those who can carry a message to Garcia.*

*Let us drop a tear, for the men who are striving to carry on a great enterprise, whose working hours are not limited by the whistle, and whose hair is fast turning white through the struggle to hold the line in dowdy indifference, slipshod imbecility, and the heartless ingratitude which, but for their enterprise, would be both hungry and homeless.*

*I wish to speak a word of sympathy for the man who succeeds — the man who, against great odds, has directed the efforts of others. There is no excellence, per se, in poverty; rags are no recommendation.*

*My heart goes out to the man who does his work when the "boss" is away, as well as when he is home. And the man who, when given a letter for Garcia, quietly takes the missive, without asking any idiotic questions, and with no lurking intention of chucking it into the nearest sewer, or of doing aught else but deliver it, never gets 'laid off', nor has to go on strike for higher wages. Civilization is one long anxious search for just such individuals. Anything such a man asks will be granted; his kind is so rare that no employer can afford to let him go. He is wanted in every city, town, and village — in every office, shop, store and factory. The world cries out for such; he is needed, and needed badly—the man who can*

*Carry a message to Garcia.*

---

This is the 12th non-habit. Buddy, if that's you, I need you right now.

*This eBook is for the use of anyone, anywhere, at no cost, and with almost no restrictions whatsoever. You may copy it, give it away, or re-use it under the terms of the Project Gutenberg License included with this eBook.*

## THE PROJECT GUTENBERG eBOOK OF A MESSAGE TO GARCIA, BY ELBERT HUBBARD[7]

### Direct download link

*No sign-in or email address required*

https://book.11ceohabits.com/bookfunnelgarcia

*Up next* 👉 *The Secret KPIs*

The CEO measures you against secret KPIs, but won't tell you till you are on par. And maybe not even then.

# CHAPTER 14
# THE SECRET KPIS

# THE SECRET KPIs

Secret KPIs have, um… a secret life. The HR department cannot access them. Because secret KPIs cannot be measured.

Secret KPIs are linked to individual traits and behaviors that drive organizational performance and market leadership. Like gems and crystals beneath the earth's surface, individuals who meet these KPIs are rare and precious.

The **CEO** measures you against these metrics, but won't tell you till you meet them. And maybe not even then.

---

*Up next* ☛ *Secret KPI — Internal Locus of Control*

Internal locus of control is a highly valued trait in organizational psychology, combat psychology, and sports psychology.

# SECRET KPI
# INTERNAL LOCUS
# OF CONTROL

The term 'internal locus of control' defies explanation unless you have an example — Anne Sullivan[1] and her student Helen Keller[2].

**HELEN KELLER** was born deaf and blind. This means she could not speak, hear or see. She overcame these limitations to be an author, political activist, and lecturer.

**ANNE SULLIVAN** was the teacher and lifelong companion to Helen Keller. Anne contracted eye disease at age five and was visually impaired. She spent a large part of her childhood in dismal living conditions. However, it did not dampen her fiery spirit. A series of eye operations significantly improved Anne's vision. She graduated from the Perkins School for the Blind at age 20 and became a teacher to Helen Keller. She taught alphabets, words and sentences by connecting language to Helen Keller's world. Anne managed the curiosity, tantrums and defiance of Helen Keller with love, steadfastness and patience.

Watch The Miracle Worker — Helen's First Lesson[3] (2:39 mins)

Helen Keller and Anne Sullivan ate impossible for breakfast. They pushed through adversity that many would consider insurmountable.

Like **Roger Bannister**[4], who broke the 4 minute barrier.

Bill Taylor says[5], "Bannister was an outlier and iconoclast — a full-time student who had little use for coaches and devised his own system for preparing to race. The British press constantly ran stories criticizing his 'lone wolf' approach, Bryant notes[6], and urged him to adopt a more conventional regimen of training and coaching".

## LOCUS OF CONTROL

Locus of control is an individual's belief system about what drives success and failure. An individual who makes lemonade from life's lemons at a neat profit to boot, has an internal locus of control.

## INTERNAL LOCUS OF CONTROL

Roger Bannister, Helen Keller, and Anne Sullivan are individuals with internal locus of control.

Organizational psychology, combat psychology, and sports psychology acknowledge internal locus of control as a highly valued trait.

In sports and combat, the opponent studies your moves and maneuvers; and finds ways to take you down. Without internal locus of control, you would not make a goal or survive the first round of swordsmanship.

In business, there is always someone with a better or cheaper product, higher marketing budget, more feet on the ground, or more years of market leadership; competing with you. The chips are stacked against you. Without internal locus of control, you are finished before you start.

## EXTERNAL LOCUS OF CONTROL

An individual whose life is a saga of helplessness against circumstances has an external locus of control. Employees with external locus of control are a source of consternation[7] to the organization.

A salesperson had this grievance to share about his product portfolio, "Product A is priced high — customers are buying the competitor's Product B because it costs less. They don't care about quality or brand equity." So, the sales person sourced the 'right' product — Product C. Sales remained poor. His grievance, "Product C is a low-cost, 'unknown' product; customers are buying the competitor's Product D because they want the best and top-of-the-line features. Price is not a problem because they want a world famous brand."

I kid you not. The sales manager did not realize the pole positions he took to justify poor sales.

---

*Up next ☛ Secret KPI — Critical Thinking*

Critical thinking makes an employee indispensable to the organization.

SECRET KPI

# CRITICAL THINKING

A Stanford report[8] says, "Our 'digital natives' may flit between Facebook and Twitter while simultaneously uploading a selfie on Instagram and texting a friend. But in evaluating information that flows through social media channels, they are easily duped."

Stanford History Education Group conducted the assessment[9] of ***civic online reasoning*** — *ability to judge the credibility of information that floods young people's smartphones, tablets, and computers.* It administered 56 tasks to students across 12 US states and analyzed 7804 responses. The sites for field testing spanned the spectrum of qualitative metrics — from under-resourced schools to well-resourced schools, from universities like Stanford (which reject 94% of its applicants) to large state universities that admit a majority of the students that apply.

The report concluded, "Overall, young people's ability to reason about the information on the internet is summed up in one word: *bleak.*"

## WHAT'S THE BIG DEAL ABOUT CRITICAL THINKING?

Critical thinking means knowing the *algorithm* of what could happen when you take a particular *action* and having a Plan A, Plan B for each of the possible outcomes.

In other words, critical thinking is having a sense of how the butterfly effect[10] plays out in your business environment.

A study[11] by MindEdge[12] shares that 64% of millennials thought critical thinking skills are important for their future job prospects. Yet, only 36% of millennials felt they are well-trained in this area, even though most studied the subject in college.

## CRITICAL THINKING MAKES AN EMPLOYEE INDISPENSABLE TO THE ORGANIZATION

The employee with critical thinking skills can solve problems, gather and analyze information, draw appropriate conclusions from data. She communicates ideas clearly and effectively via email, one-on-one, within a group, during a cold call, and in high-stakes meetings with external stakeholders. Critical thinking allows her to process incoming information and relay corresponding messages. These messages trigger a cascade of events leading to desired outcomes.

Some employees are natural critical thinkers. These employees get hand-picked for high-stakes assignments. The assignments could be — soothing a hostile customer, getting a payment released from a key account, converting a customer who prefers the competitor's product, and negotiating terms with a supplier.

*Up next* ☛ *Secret KPI — Contrastive Detail Management*

Contrastive detail creates a favorable first impression.

# SECRET KPI
# CONTRASTIVE DETAIL MANAGEMENT

Contrastive detail management means spotting and fixing errors *before* stuff goes to the printer, web page, blog, press release, to a meeting or intranet.

Contrastive detail creates a favorable first impression. It smoothes the path to building credibility and stakeholder trust. Yet, the casual attitude towards contrastive detail in front-end communications is appalling. Document management tools such as Auto correct, Spell checker, Thesaurus, Hemingway Editor[13], ProWritingAid[14], Grammarly[15], drag-and-drop publishing, and free online tutorials are accessible. Yet, it is common to see emails, resumé, reports, brochures, press releases, and web pages with errors, typos, layout nightmares, grammatical no-nos[16] and creative harakiri[17].

*Death by error and typo overload*

## MIND THE FRONT END OF COMMUNICATION

The front end of communication is stuff that is sent to external stakeholders. It conveys the culture and competence of the organization. If you mess up here, external stakeholders won't know you are the cat's whiskers. There isn't a teacher looking over your shoulder or grading assignments at the workplace. Be your own auditor.

---

*Up next* ☛ *Secret KPI — Resilience*

Resilience is an invaluable gift that the CEO acknowledges with gratitude.

# SECRET KPI
# RESILIENCE

Resilience means absorbing the impact of personal adversity, group trauma and organizational mishaps in real-time, with a minimal decline in clarity of thought.

## A GIFT TO THE CEO

A resilient employee is a gift that the hands-on CEO accepts with grace and gratitude. Because no one knows how resilience is built.

While it's not clear how to *be* resilient, individuals with resilience exhibit certain traits and behaviors. Resilient individuals have a heightened awareness of the mind-body connection. They use the mind to control the body and vice versa. They observe their emotions with selective detachment while being immersed in it. They place their emotions on hold, attend to a deadline, and resume the emotional journey that is important to their inner world. They pick up and drop the thread of a grieving process at will, do justice to their outer and inner world, align and calibrate physiological responses to the priorities of the moment. They move fast or stay glued to their seat — adapting quickly to whichever action meets the need of the hour.

The resilient employee will invariably enter the Hands-On CEO's inner circle.

## WHAT RESILIENCE ISN'T

Blog writers, authors and organizations (who weave 'resilience' into the mission statement) seem to be enamored by the word and it bears clarification. Resilience is not the same as 'character', 'quick recovery', 'coping', 'bouncing back' or 'adapting to circumstances'.

A dangerous notion exists that resilience is built through adversity. It is a misconception that challenges build resilience. On the contrary, challenges in quick succession crumble resilience.

## THE RESILIENCE — INTERNAL LOCUS OF CONTROL CONNECTION

Resilient employees have internal locus of control. Their premise is that they, not their circumstances, control behavior.

Author, Psychologist and Blog Writer Maria Konnikova[18] shares in the blog article 'How People Learn to Become Resilient[19]', "Resilience is demonstrated at a young age. A thirty-two-year longitudinal project followed six hundred ninety-eight children from pre-birth through their third decade of life. Resilient children saw themselves as the orchestrators of their own fates. They tend to 'meet the world on their own terms'. On a scale that measured locus of control, they scored more than two standard deviations away from the standardization group."

*Up next* 👉 *Secret KPI — Closing the Loop*

Employees that close the loop are placed in supervisory and project management roles.

SECRET KPI
CLOSING THE
LOOP

Closing the loop means taking a chain of communication or actions to its natural conclusion and keeping stakeholders informed.

Employees that close the loop are quickly placed in supervisory and project management roles. As newbies, they will overtake colleagues that have supervisory experience and certifications in project management.

---

*Up next* ☛ *Secret KPI — Quantum Leaper*

The quantum leaper restores the momentum and pace of operations.

## SECRET KPI
# QUANTUM LEAPER

A quantum leap is a dramatic jump from one energy state to another. You are a quantum leaper if you manage negative disruptions and keep things moving on schedule.

Examples of negative disruptions are assembly line malfunction close to a shipment deadline, wrong parts received for a device being launched next week, traffic control challenge on the freeway because of a freak accident during peak hours.

The quantum leaper shifts mental gears on the fly, to restore the momentum and pace of operations. He makes quantum leaps in creative problem solving, contingency management, and stakeholder communications.

## THE NEED FOR A QUANTUM LEAPER

The SOPs[20] of an organization do not cover every contingency. Sometimes there is not enough time and no one to ask *What do we do now?* A quantum leaper doesn't require permission to think and will do what needs to be done.

* * *

*Up next* ☛ *Secret KPI — Will Work for Free*

Companies that survive crises have people who would work for free.

# SECRET KPI
# WILL WORK FOR FREE

Did you raise a brow to this one? Think about the time you helped a friend complete a DIY project, answered a technical question on Quora, or posted a life hack video online. It was fun, gratifying, and you would do it again.

If this is you, you are likely to stay on the sinking ship of an organization and plug the holes.

The global pandemic of 2020 has placed this secret KPI in the spotlight. As entrepreneurs and businesses struggled; the layoffs, pay cuts and delayed paychecks hit people hard. Giant corporations declared bankruptcy, international businesses sank. Companies that survived the crisis had a team of can-do-will-do-whatever-needs-to-be-done people.

The organization is a living organism that needs people who care. When an organization is in trouble, some people refuse to leave.

At the closure of the rough ride experienced by scandal-bogged Finablr[21], Bhairav Trivedi said[22], "Our employees have worked at reduced or zero pay for some months and this acquisition deal is only possible thanks to their hard work and sacrifice."

*Up next* ☛ *Secret KPI — Don't Make Me Think*

Who thinks for you?

# SECRET KPI
# DON'T MAKE ME
# THINK

You are hired to think, not just 'do stuff'. When you don't think, someone else must think for you.

You are not pulling your weight in the organization if someone else must think for you, provide direction, give feedback, pump encouragement, steer alignment, perform calibration and appraisal.

Your supervisor or line manager is not there to think for you, he is there to develop the territory and support organizational strategy. Are you pulling your weight?

---

*Up next* ☞ *Secret KPI — Gratitude*

Gratitude makes economic sense.

# SECRET KPI
# GRATITUDE

The law of diminishing returns says that when a person uses a product, service or reward again and again, the satisfaction derived from it keeps declining.

It's the difference between the first bite of food when hunger strikes and every subsequent bite. The sensory gratification is highest in the beginning and diminishes as hunger is satiated.

## THE DIFFERENCE BETWEEN DIMINISHING RETURNS AND GRATITUDE

Gratitude is different.

It is a state of consciousness that values the product, service or reward consistently across time.

## GRATITUDE IN BUSINESS

In business, lack of gratitude creates economic problems that have no easy answers. The economic issues linked to lack of gratitude — customers want to pay less each time they make a repeat purchase, manufacturers want to price the product more each time a loyal customer returns; clients shop for cheaper, better spa services even though they are happy with the current service provider; the next smartphone release has features that you *must* have.

The culture of ingratitude increases the carbon footprint of nations, landfills proliferate, air is polluted, and businesses must work 24/7 to stay in the game.

Gratitude is the hedge against a 'want more' culture that creates lifelong debt.

At the workplace, employees with gratitude are happy, productive and consistent across the ups and downs of work and life. Without gratitude, employees see what they don't have and lose sight of what they have. The imbalance distorts their view of reality and judgment across workplace decisions. It leads to underperformance, dissatisfaction and poor decision-making.

---

*Up next* ☛ *The CEO's Inner Circle*

The CEO's Inner Circle is everything you imagine it to be.

# CHAPTER 15
# THE CEO'S INNER CIRCLE

The CEO's Inner Circle is everything you imagine it to be. It is a haven that grants you salient power and efficient closures on the agenda.

What the CEO's Inner circle isn't — a clique, mafia or a cauldron of secret motives.

## INNER CIRCLE TRAITS

The CEO's Inner Circle comprises people with *Inner Circle Traits.*

The traits are wisdom, defiance, dependability and ability to think beyond the self.

Isn't every employee supposed to be dependable? Aren't humans *engineered* to think beyond the self?

In theory, yes. In reality, it is rare.

## THE JOURNEY TO THE CEO'S INNER CIRCLE

Your journey into the CEO's Inner Circle starts with behaviors and actions that demonstrate alignment with organizational interests, mission and vision. This is where many fail.

Those who pass the litmus test invariably demonstrate one or more of the inner circle traits. These individuals do not care about being in the CEO's Inner Circle. It is the CEO who is grateful to have them on the team.

---

*Up next* ☛ *Inner Circle Trait — Wisdom*

Same as intelligence?

CEO'S INNER CIRCLE
# WISDOM

The 'happening word' of the 21st century is intelligence. Are you intelligent or wise?

## INTELLIGENCE AND WISDOM

A question was posed on Quora — Which do you prefer: wisdom or intelligence? Reader responses[1] to the question illustrate the difference between wisdom[2] and intelligence.[3]

Quora Contributor Daniel Paterson says, *"Now, sure knowledge (intelligence) can bring you to some places, but even if you're the smartest person in the world, without wisdom and common sense, you'll be dumber than a wise person. And that's only because wise people will help others and know what to do in life. Those who don't have wisdom just… won't.*

*Let's take, for instance, you're on a boat cruise that's crashing. If you're wise, without being smart, then you:*

*• Choose to help others, along with finding the emergency escape room to get everybody out. You make sure that everyone is safe, and the boat sinks with no casualties.*

*If you're smart without being wise, then you:*

*• Calculate the velocity and acceleration of the boat sinking and the chances of your survival. You may craft a raft, or something like that, to save yourself, after calculating the chances of survival.*

*◦ But how long is that calculation going to take? You can't keep calculating — the boat's sinking!*

◦ *Even if you use your intelligence to find the Emergency Escape Room, more casualties may occur because you're more invested in your own survival than the survival of everyone around you.*

*Now, let's apply that to everyday life — someone scrapes their knee.*

◦ *Wise person: comfort them and help them heal with bandages.*

◦ *Smart person: you may help them heal with the right salve, but it's not certain. Plus, you won't comfort them.*

*Smart people learn from their own mistakes. Wise people learn from other's mistakes and never make those mistakes in the first place. Finally, it takes a wise person to answer this question — but not a smart person ."*

## WISDOM IS A VIRTUE

Semantic Technologist, Researcher, and Quora contributor, Anne Cregan[4] says, *"Intelligence is the ability to reason and acquire knowledge, whilst Wisdom is the ability to apply that reasoning ability / knowledge, synthesize it with other utility-based things and produce useful / 'good' real world outcomes. A very important question to answer is "Useful to who?" and the consensus seems to be that Wisdom leans towards public good rather than individual gain. In my book, that is a really good thing ."*

Scholar and Professor Ivan William Kelly[5] says, *"Wisdom is a virtue[6]. Intelligent criminals are possible, but wise criminals are ruled out by definition[7]."*

The CEO's Inner Circle has wise persons who are generalists and specialists at the same time. When combined with the other inner circle traits, they are one-man armies, the trump[8] card in a deck, the knight[9] of a chess game. You must recognize and spot wisdom because these folks hide their light under a bushel.[10]

---

*Up next* ☛ *Inner Circle Trait — Dependability*

How would *you* handle a hostage negotiation?

CEO'S INNER CIRCLE

# DEPEND ABILITY

The CEO defines dependability as the ability to lead a critical mission that is constrained by a high degree of uncertainty.

Often, the dependable individual leads the mission with limited experience of atleast some aspect of the task, stakeholders, or the ecosystem.

For example, hostage negotiations.

Author and ex-FBI agent Chris Voss narrates a hostage incident in the book 'Never Split The Difference', "In August 2000, a militant group took a hostage and put a $10 million tag on his head. The negotiating adversary was a terrorist-sociopath-killer with a history of rape, murder, and beheadings. He liked to record his deeds on video and send it to the media."

How would *you* handle it?

Think about the scenario and success objectives.

The goal of hostage negotiations is to free the hostage without harm and if possible, have the hostage taker surrender peacefully. This is easier said than done. The immediacy of the task is undeniable, the stakes are high, lives hang in balance.

You need a hostage negotiator with a track record of dependability. Read the book 'Never Split The Difference' to know the outcomes of the hostage incident and the negotiation rules that helped free the hostage (Hey, did you think I would share the spoiler?).

Consider these critical missions — a multi-million dollar bid qualification meeting, international cooperation between hostile nations, ethical disclosure of sentinel[11] events to healthcare authorities, announcing a global product recall to consumers, distributors and shareholders.

These are situations that can only be described as — *until you know what you are dealing with, you don't know what you are dealing with.* There is no standard formula for managing these complex situations, and the cost of failure is high.

That's why you need dependability. Not to assure textbook outcomes, but to assure the best outcomes in that *unique* situation.

Dependable persons think on their feet, establish credibility quickly and secure buy-in for desired outcomes.

The **CEO**'s Inner Circle has dependable persons who convert real-time[12] learning into real-time application. They know what good looks like and can make the right choices as the drama unfolds.

*Up next ☛ Inner Circle Trait — Defiance*

Defiance is a driver of performance and excellence.

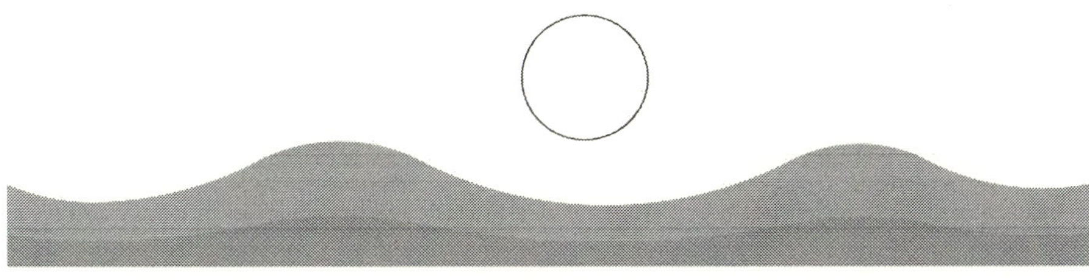

CEO'S INNER CIRCLE

# DEFIANCE

No breakthrough was ever achieved without a spirit of defiance. Like a wild steed who grows to love you, the individual with defiance leads the organization through rough terrain. He *is* the one who would carry a message to Garcia[13].

Defiance is central to organizational excellence. The defiant are not shy to shoot down the CEO's pet projects if they are flawed. They don't get a kick out of being in the CEO's Inner Circle.

They dance to their own drummer[14] and would leave the job if it is in the interest of the organization. For you see, they create their world wherever they go.

---

*Up next ☛ Inner Circle Trait — Ability to think beyond the self*

Surprise, it is not what you think.

CEO'S INNER CIRCLE
ABILITY TO THINK
BEYOND
THE
SELF

The ability to think beyond the self requires you to have values bigger than yourself. In a 'me-first culture', this seems like a big deal.

The scientific term for the ability to think beyond the self is self-transcendence.

Research Director at the Annenberg School for Communication, Yoona Kang[15] says, "People report that self-transcendence is an intrinsically rewarding experience[16]."

Self-transcendence isn't about saving the world or volunteering for a cause. It is closer to home. It is practiced *at the workplace*.

Do you help colleagues? Do you stay late at the office to meet a deadline? Good for you if you do. But that is not self-transcendence, either.

Self-transcendence is being punctual for a team meeting, not late. It is keeping your colleagues in the loop; it is inter-departmental collaboration; it is capping your manipulation and sabotage tendencies; it is respect for the back office team; it is minimizing last minute requests for resources; it is performing self-audit; it is dropping the 'act' and being authentic; it is the courage to see your gaps and the strengths of colleagues; it is taming your envy, jealousy and callousness; it is knowing that you are here to serve before you take your 'rightful due'.

Viktor Frankl[17] survived the Holocaust and spent his life helping others find meaning in life. You would expect philosophical advice from his experience of human suffering. Instead, he has this to say.

> A man who is conscious of the responsibility towards another human being affectionately waiting for him; or conscious of the responsibility towards an unfinished work; will never be able to throw away his life. He knows the 'why' for his existence, and will be able to bear almost any 'how'[18]. ~ Viktor Frankl[19], Man's Search for Meaning[20], p. 101

The individuals who think beyond the self are ushered into the CEO's inner circle with eagerness and gratitude.

*Up next* ☛ *The Hidden Side of the Organization*

Every organization has a hidden side. You knew that, right?

# PART III

# CHAPTER 16

# THE HIDDEN SIDE OF THE ORGANIZATION

The hidden side of the organization reveals itself in the first few months on the job. It feels as if someone has pulled the rug from under your feet.

You tell yourself, "There is a layer of information I didn't see before. I am afraid to dig deep. Landing this job was a milestone, and I just want to breathe easy for a while. I can't quit and start another job hunt. Maybe it's my imagination. Don't be negative, think positive."

Sounds sinister. But it isn't really (okay, that's a lie).

The next few pages will decode the stuff.

---

*Up next* ☛ *The Grayscale Employee*

The grayscale employee spans the spectrum — from the mundane to the sinister.

# THE GRAYSCALE EMPLOYEE

# THE GRAYSCALE EMPLOYEE

T he nurse asked whether she could leave early if the patient didn't make it to the next day. *He didn't.*

## WHEN HEALERS TURN KILLERS

In an exposé that chills to the bone, Author Katherine Ramsland[1], author of Inside The Minds Of Healthcare Serial Killers — Why they kill[2] & John Camp[3], author of One Hundred Years Of

Medical Murder[4], reveal serial killers in healthcare. As you read the true stories, the lack of situational awareness exhibited by hospital staff and the failure to spot black swans makes the jaw drop.

The dark pursuits of surgeons, physicians, nurses and orderly staff remained hidden in plain sight, in some cases, for over two decades.

These serial killers in healthcare moved from one institution to another, leaving behind an elevated death count and gaping holes in the well-being of numerous families.

Katherine Ramsland[5] says, *"No hospital, nursing home or healthcare facility would knowingly ignore a killer on the team, but the nature of healthcare and the constant demands on the system inadvertently provide an avenue for predators. Hospitals*

*must acknowledge their existence, train personnel to spot them, document their movements, and take action, both before and after crimes occur. It's not easy for anyone to accept that a co-worker might actually be a killer, and it's hard to be a whistle-blower based on suspicion alone. However, the arrest and conviction of healthcare employees since the 1970s has led criminologists and psychologists to conclude that these offenders occupy a special subcategory among serial killers."*

She emphasizes the need to involve the law and clearly communicate 'do not rehire' information in the background check feedback to hospitals. Because of the fear of being sued, many supervisors did not disclose their reservations to the future employer, though they withheld positive feedback. She shares the red flags to look for.

If you run a healthcare facility, these books must be in the library of the CEO's office.

**Inside The Minds Of Healthcare Serial Killers**[6] **— Why they kill.** By Katherine Ramsland

**One Hundred Years Of Medical Murder**[7]. By John Camp

When people with dysfunctional tendencies and 'a touch of the devil' enter the caregiver workforce, CEO Habits #6, #7, #8, #10 become critical to the safety of its stakeholders.

## WHITE COLLAR CRIME THAT NEEDED FBI INTERVENTION

Ordinary-guy-turned-FBI-agent, Author John W. Schilling reveals the insurance billing fraud perpetrated by Hospital Corporation of America[8] in the book '**Undercover**[9] **— How I went from company man to FBI spy and exposed the worst healthcare fraud in US history**'. It took years of undercover work to compile the evidence and nail the offenders. The federal probe is one of the longest and costliest investigations for healthcare fraud in US history.

## OPPORTUNITY AND CAMOUFLAGE

In both the crime categories, serial killing spree and insurance billing scam, the grayscale employees exploited circumstantial factors — ease of opportunity and ease of camouflage. It was easy for them to commit the crime and get away with it. And a human factor aided the crimes — conscientious colleagues decided not to think about what was happening, because it was beyond the 'scope' of their job description.

## MISALIGNMENT

In business, the grayscale employee creates situations misaligned with organizational interests.

THE GARDEN-VARIETY[10] GRAYSCALE EMPLOYEE takes office stationery home, or pockets an item classified as dead stock[11]. He bills a drink-too-many to the company account and pads fuel expenses each month.

These employees are a minor nuisance to the organization. They may exhibit grayscale behavior in transient moments of weakness, but the behavior could also be the tip of a sinister iceberg. Employees often justify garden-variety grayscale behavior (in their mind) as 'compensation' for another expense that is not billable. The administration team must keep an eye on them and plug the easy-opportunity-easy-camouflage gaps within organizational infrastructure.

THE DEADWOOD[12] GRAYSCALE EMPLOYEE uses the singularity of the team to avoid individual accountability. Such employees trickle into the organization steadily (HR processes are not equipped to predict the behavior) and trickle out naturally when the behavior becomes too obvious to ignore.

Blogger Barbara Bartlein says in the blog article 'Dealing with energy-sucking 'deadwood' employees[13]', "*No matter what the individual circumstances are, deadwood affects the momentum of the team. Such employees become "energy-suckers," bringing everyone else down. Energy suckers can sabotage a whole area, sprinkling negativity in their path. Other team members may feel discouraged as they see their own efforts receiving little positive attention while the deadwood gets away with poor performance.*"

*The sinister grayscale employee reminds you of the sea faring bandit*

A BREED OF SINISTER[14] GRAYSCALE EMPLOYEES aim to take root in the organization and sap its energy. The motive is to fund personal plans at the expense of the organization. This could be an entrepreneurial venture with conflict of interest, a home mortgage or steady disposable income. They build a nexus of contacts to serve them when they move on or are caught red-handed. When they leave the organization, they plot ways to make the organization bleed.

The decision to let them go is like being stuck between a rock and a hard place. The CEO must decide what is in the best interest of the organization on a case-to-case basis. If you have a mechanism to prune his power within the organization, he can be managed as a snake-up-the-sleeve. If you are able to cap the grayscale employee's influence with external stakeholders when he is no longer a part of the organization, the dismissal must be swift.

## TEAM DYNAMICS AND RIVALRY

Team dynamics and rivalry expose the weaker side of human nature. As a manger, newbie and intern, your morale may be derailed by grayscale employees who

⊙ Sabotage your project

⊙ Distort information and relay it to your line manager

⊙ Manipulate working relationships for personal gain

⊙ Give you assignments that are guaranteed to fail

⊙ Shun you if you refrain from gossip

⊙ Run a micro-organization or fiefdom[15] within the company; you remain an outsider unless you 'join the gang'

## MOTIVATIONS

How to deal with the grayscale employee?

You can deal with him once you uncover his motivations and when you know what rubs him the wrong way[16]. It may be that

↘ He is planning to join the competitor so wants the project to fail

- Your competence shows him in a poor light
- Something he said can't-be-done without a huge budget was done by you in a couple of days using free apps
- They are dead wood and your ideas create actual work for them
- They see you as someone who could replace them
- Plain envy, because they feel they couldn't be you even if they tried
- They want to replace you with their cousin
- You exposed their flawed judgment inadvertently on a public forum
- You created a profitable account with a customer that declined to do business with him in the past
- It's not about you. You are simply caught in the rivalry between two individuals, or someone has a stake in keeping people at conflict with each other.

## YOUR OPTIONS

Once you know the motivations, you can assess your options

- Quit the job if the sh*t is knee deep and you dread each day at work.
- Mobilize a lateral shift to another department or role if the hostility relates to current position.

❀ If either of above options is not possible, bide your time, update your resume and keep your spiritual core recharged.

❀ Slow down the 'game' by shifting into neutral gear and lying low. Look for Black Swans that lend weight to your voice and shift circumstances in your favor.

❀ Escalate the matter to someone you trust is an option. Senior management may be aware of the problem and looking for further evidence. But it is also possible they do not believe you, or you could be perceived as part of the problem.

❀ Lifescripts[17] could be used to manage difficult conversations if you choose to confront the grayscale employee.

## THE CORPORATE CON MAN

The corporate con man is the ultimate grayscale employee. You can't decide whether he is a boon or a bane. Nothing is sacred to him. His charm, aggression and show of control leave you in awe.

The corporate con man baffles the system. He has massive competencies and massive character flaws. He uses the competencies to establish arm-twister influence. His business decisions are self-serving but projected as business acumen. The facade of the corporate con man drops easily, but he is adept at putting it back up.

Colleagues who recognize the damage caused by the corporate con man wonder, *"Why is this person in the company? How can the company let him get away with this behavior?"*

He lacks integrity, empathy, and self-awareness. But it is surprising how easily the corporate con convinces everyone that the character flaws are leadership traits.

The corporate con man is uncovered when a white collar crime makes the company bleed.

Paul Babiak and Robert D. Hare[18] say, "Unfortunately, even an organization with sophisticated hiring and promotion practices would find it challenging to defend itself against these 'corporate cons'. Even loyal employees who are first-hand witnesses to the machinations do not truly understand what is happening. And when some do raise the red flag, they may find no one at the top responds to it."

---

*Up next ☛ Personal Power*

Personal power shapes choices and life experiences.

# CHAPTER 18
# PERSONAL POWER

Personal power is systematically curbed from the moment of birth. Being nursed on schedule rather than demand; sitting on the potty, going to bed, and waking up on a schedule as prep for academic life; completing homework *before* play time; cramming for exams; being nice to the nosy neighbor; the list goes on — these are common childhood experiences.

It is called discipline. The discipline is achieved by trading in the child's personal power. The power to decide. The power to say no.

The rewards of validation, hugs and parental approval (or punishment in abusive environments) provide the momentum to embrace the discipline. You internalize the discipline and realize it's all for good (or good intentions, at least). And things hum along smoothly.

Adolescence brings an immense urge to reclaim personal power. It alarms you and those around you. There is rebellion, guilt and confusion. Adolescence coincides with campus life, a new set of friends, perspectives different from your own, and nasty people who wreck your feelings. Personal power takes a beating once again.

By trial and error, you and your family nurture your personal power. You learn how to assert yourself, exercise judgment, and communicate your premise.

## PERSONAL POWER AND LIFE CHOICES

Personal power shapes choices and life experiences. It is intrinsically connected to survival.

I was young when my mother passed away. I miss her and imagine how it would be to take a deep breath and inhale the presence of 'mom' again.

I didn't enjoy going to school and wondered what it took to be rich. Hard times came by when dad was bedridden. Ever the 'man of the house', he continued to guide our decisions and manage affairs of the home. Dad was my mentor. He taught me sales etiquette, how to win trust, and how to achieve daily targets.

An incident occurred that shaped my life. A close relative running a successful trading enterprise offered to hire me. The remuneration was exploitative ( = peanuts). I flew into a rage; no one deserved to be treated like this. Talk about being dramatic. I promised myself that *I* would pay my team well (in case you are curious; it is a promise I have kept).

In hindsight, I understand what ticked me off. The low-ball offer was a ploy to erode my personal power. Low-balling[1] is an effective negotiation strategy, but not in talent management.

## PERSONAL POWER AT THE WORKPLACE

For some of us, the family may have a vested interest in keeping your personal power under check. Pathological possessiveness, cultural legacy, sibling issues, control tendencies, Munchausen syndrome[2], and Munchausen-by-proxy[3] may be ploys to keep you weak, restricted and dependent. When this happens, your attempts to nurture personal power become 'unreasonable requests' that upset the applecart of family.

If you enter the workplace with compromised personal power, the grayscale employee finds you easy prey. His wily ways keep your personal power at rock bottom. Talent and sincerity brings career stability, but it's an arduous and dismal journey.

Even if you have a healthy reservoir of personal power, the grayscale employee has a plan to trim it. If there isn't a grayscale employee around, organizations create natural conditions that place personal power at risk.

Your job is to reclaim and protect your personal power. Team dynamics, and relative power depend upon it.

## ASSESS YOUR PERSONAL POWER

Self-appraisal will reveal whether personal power is compromised. It may be the case if

✪ You repeat the same sentences during a conversation, verbal reporting or team huddle. It's as if you think people don't hear you the first time.

✪ You are blindsided by rude responses, veiled threats and passive aggressive events.

✪ You wonder why a colleague ignores your emails, but hesitate to ask.

✪ You are extra nice to those who have been nasty to you.

✪ You do not spot sabotage-at-work till it's too late or pointed out to you.

✪ You wonder why being talented, transparent and dedicated is not enough to gain buy-in from the team.


## THE TOUGH TRUTH

You give away your power. No one can steal it without your permission.

Listen to my colleague, *"As a child, I had a reservoir of personal power, fierce determination and a worldview different from the collective worldview of my family. My mother was a source of strength and direction, but extreme circumstances transformed her from a visionary leader to a fearful, controlling matriarch. Differences of opinion were not tolerated, and met with stinging criticism and ridicule. I had a decision to make — fall in line with mother's worldview or add to mother's emotional pain through behavior that she does not understand. I chose to fall in line. To do so, I had to put my personal power to sleep. The crush-the-rebellion war that I waged against myself was so successful that I lost all sense of self. I could not differentiate between what I liked and disliked, what I wanted or not. The self became a flat line[4] of such proportions, that mother would ask what I want for the day's meal, so she could plan accordingly. I could not answer, I had no idea what I wanted. Curiously, the lack of personal power did not affect productivity, joie de vivre and belief in the ability to do great things. Go figure. But it messed up my relationship-building skills. I could not establish the algorithm of mutual respect, holding my own within a group and synergy in relationships. As I look back, lack of personal power probably precipitated a failed marriage, workplace woes and aversion to tasks that require teamwork."*

This colleague is a talented technocrat, but had massive blind spots on reclaiming and protecting personal power at the workplace. Several years ago, I pointed out the persons who were sabotaging her efforts in the organization. Her inner radar was not equipped to pick up the information.

Similarly, individuals who endure sustained domestic violence, incest and sexual abuse barter personal power for the stability and protection of family members. A human responds to danger with a fight-or-flight response. It is our primary survival tool. Enduring abuse requires a no-fight-no-flight-stay-there-change-nothing response. This is so contrary to human engineering that it can only be achieved through dissociation[5] with the self. The dissociation handicaps your ability to protect personal power.

## WHAT'S GOING ON?

The vulnerability to loss of personal power is high in the first few months of a new job.

This is when things happen that leave you bewildered.

◎ You speak up at a meeting and the room grows quiet. Did you say something wrong?

◎ You present a suggestion and it is acknowledged but ignored. What's wrong with the suggestion?

◎ There are people in the company whose roles don't align with their formal designation. How do you respond to them?

◎ Decisions are changed by your line manager abruptly, without an obvious reason (at least to you). Why won't your line manager tell you?

◎ The matrix of power and hierarchy turns out to be complex, it's not the cocooned world of you-and-your-line-manager. Who are the people whose buy-in is crucial?

◎ Your job does not match the job description. When will you get to do what the offer letter describes?

◎ A colleague refuses to cooperate. You are still a newbie; how did you get on his wrong side so soon?

◎ You are in charge on paper, but someone else must approve each micro-step. How would you make the progress envisaged in the beginning?

◎ You request historical data of departmental performance and get evasive replies. How are you supposed to establish **KPIs** without baseline measurement?

◎ There is a 'CEO's darling' on the team. How do you report his contribution to a recent screw up?

◎ You discover that your line manager does not have industry experience or the knowledge, skills and abilities for the job. You have become his external brain and personal assistant. Why is he the line manager? Does the organization not care about its interests?

◎ You assess that processes and systems critical to departmental performance are not in place. You are told that it's all about how *you* perform, processes don't deliver results, humans do. How do you shift the focus from your performance to departmental performance?

◎ Your subordinates ignore instructions. When confronted, they say you are making a big deal of a trivial issue. Why don't they follow the instructions?

◎ You approach a colleague to address silo syndrome and seek inter-departmental cooperation. He agrees, but the initiatives never take off. He's been too busy lately (like forever). Why won't he cooperate?

With no straightforward answers, bills to pay, and glowing LinkedIn congratulations bursting through your inbox, you dread going on a job hunt again. Maybe things will get better with time. You 'zone out' and stop thinking. Welcome to zombie land.

## THE WORKPLACE ZOMBIE

As a workplace zombie, here is some stuff you do

➤ You know the project is screwed from the beginning. But you stay quiet.

➤ You see an initiative as 'too little, too late'. But you applaud the team and cheer for them.

❧    A simple tweak can improve a process. But you look the other way.

❧    Your company initiates the Great Place To Work [6]Certification™. It is anything but a great place to work. You raise your hand to lead the project.

None of these behaviors serve the organization. The qualitative loss to the organization is high. Yet, there aren't effective measures to address these workplace woes.

## BEWARE OF VEXATION

Loss of personal power is not caused by individual events. It happens when a state of sustained vexation is generated by a stack up of events. Vexation is a feeling of being puzzled, worried and frustrated at the same time. Vexation transforms your default workplace behavior from action to immobility.

Vexation is a mind control tool of the grayscale employee. Your personal power is low when you are deliberately kept in limbo[7] or on tenterhooks[8] .

Author and Blogger Shahida Arabi[9] says in the blog 20 Diversion Tactics Highly Manipulative Narcissists, Sociopaths And Psychopaths Use To Silence You[10], *"They use a plethora of diversionary tactics that distort your reality, deflect their responsibility, and silence you."*

Dark spiritual arts use vexation to weaken the aura. Vexation is a key rubric linked to mental aggravation in homeopathic case management.

## THE SOCIOPATH CONFESSES

Author M.E. Thomas is (was) a self-confirmed sociopath. She shares her own psychological evaluation report in the book 'Confessions of a Sociopath'[11], "Ms. Thomas's clinical presentation ... were pronounced elevations on scales tapping antisocial and psychopathic traits (particularly egocentrism and sensation-seeking characteristics), interpersonal dominance, verbal aggression, and excessive self-esteem, as well as very low scores on measures tapping negative affective experiences (eg., phobias, traumatic stressors, depressive symptoms), interpersonal nurturance and stressful life events. Ms. Thomas views herself as 'different' but not 'disordered'. She seems content with her lifestyle and appears to have excelled across various life domains (e.g., academic, occupational). One might describe her as a 'socialized' or 'successful' variant of the psychopathic personality pattern."

She says, "I am absolutely shameless when it comes to asking for, pushing for, and ultimately inducing people to give me what I want, whatever it takes."

M.E. Thomas is a rare grayscale individual. She has self-awareness, and has applied it in the service of good.

## NOT EVERYTHING IS AN ATTACK ON PERSONAL POWER

The workplace is prone to subterfuge, and nasty colleagues make it worse. But you must differentiate between a toxic work environment and the dynamics of organizational performance. Not everything that looks oppressive may be so.

✪ Working overtime without pay, incurring expenses that don't get reimbursed, urgent calls on weekends are not attacks on personal power. If it *is* exploitation according to the local labor regulations, raise the issue. Sometimes, organizations are penny-wise and pound-foolish. A reasonable margin exists for organizations to expect availability, and not reimburse every penny spent in the 'service' of the organization. Like the other foibles of human nature, if it is not giving you sleepless nights, move on.

Kimmie Marek, MS, Chief Creative Officer and Co-Owner at 7 Charming Sisters says in the blog article 49 Secrets Your Boss Won't Tell You—But You Need to Know[12], "Passion and grit are high commodities these days and fewer and fewer employees have it. Look at this job as more than a paycheck and I'll look at you as more than just another employee."

✪ Learn to work with hostile team members. Yes, it is possible. A project has its deliverables and plan. Maintain a visible trail of tasks and communication so that manipulation and sabotage tactics are unsuccessful. Be on time. Receive inputs with an open mind. Trash the ones aimed to hurt or harm. When providing feedback, focus on project constraints, milestones achieved, optimistic outcomes and best practices of the industry. Speak with clarity. Avoid filler words; they make you appear unsure and easy prey to the grayscale employee.

✪ Businesses are no longer local enterprises. The concept of world-as-global-village means international business is the norm rather than the exception. Working hours now overlap time zones. This means your workday is longer or erratic or both. Embrace the new world of work. Several of my colleagues work remotely with no supervision. Due to disparate time zones, the communication is via messaging and voice notes. They are accountable for deliverables, not man hours. They are on-schedule with projects. I don't have to ask; they keep me updated. I can count on them to deliver on a time-sensitive assignment. It's the credibility and personal power they have crafted.

## THE MYTH OF WORK-LIFE BALANCE

THE MYTH OF WORK-LIFE BALANCE creates the notion that work is a contained environment with norms and standards of practice. It is not. Shit happens at work. Because work *is* life.

## RECLAIMING PERSONAL POWER

REMOVE THE ELEMENT OF SURPRISE from the equation. When you recognize how loss of personal power takes place, you can pre-empt the tactics and manage the situation.

**Use Lifescripts**[13]**, Comebacks**[14]**, Black Swans**[15] to negotiate relationships and steer outcomes at the workplace.

**BUILD THE USP OF YOU** Find a way to be indispensable to those who support you and those who sabotage you. The good guys will have a stake in watching your back and bad guys will figure it is better to be friends.

**WHEN NOTHING WORKS** If the organizational culture is dragging you under, quit. Author Marie McIntyre[16] says in the book, 'Secrets to Winning at Office Politics'[17], *"When the culture seems uncomfortable or wrong, give yourself a reasonable amount of time to adjust. Then, if you still feel like a misfit, you may need to move on. Putting a person into a company is kind of like an organ transplant. Sometimes the new part turns out to be compatible, and sometimes not. Just as the body will eventually reject an incompatible organ, a company will eventually reject an incompatible member. Some transplants just don't take."*

**BIDE YOUR TIME** if you can't quit. Keep your resume updated. Pray, meditate or switch your attention. Keep yourself recharged. Seek professional counseling to receive validation for what you are going through.

**CUT THE CORD** on toxic relationships. These include friends who borrow money, clothes, makeup, friends who exert pressure to conform to the group, friends who don't understand your world and belittle your concerns. Author Shahida Arabi says in the book 'Becoming the Narcissist's Nightmare: How to Devalue and Discard the Narcissist While Supplying yourself"[18], "*Narcissistic partners engage in chronic manipulation which includes an idealization-devaluation-discard abuse cycle where they 'love bomb' their partners, devalue them, then discard them.*"

---

*Up next* ☛ *The Burning Question*

Why do bad people survive and thrive in good organizations?

# CHAPTER 19
# THE BURNING QUESTION
## WHY DO BAD PEOPLE SURVIVE AND THRIVE IN GOOD ORGANIZATIONS?

The success of an organization depends on employee morale and wellbeing. Yet, an unbelievable volume of books have been written on the subterfuge, politics, and mischief mongering raked up by toxic, narcissistic, psychopathic, evil, petty minded, manipulative people at the workplace. The problem of 'bad' people at the workplace is the elephant in the room that leaders rarely acknowledge. The workplace is supposed to foster and encourage exemplary behavior. The term 'organizational behavior'[1] is the rug under which bad behavior is swept away.

What is bad behavior anyway? And who is a bad person?

Outside of a theological framework, bad is any behavior that a person would not exhibit towards those he loves and cares about. A bad person is one who repeats the behavior in full knowledge. If you have skipped chapters to read this one, refer to the preceding chapters in Part III - The Hidden Side of the Organization, The Grayscale Employee and Personal Power.

The Grayscale Employee discusses behavior that undermines organizational interest. Personal Power discusses behavior that compromises individual and team morale.

Bad people in good organizations are the norm rather than the exception.

## GAPS THAT ALLOW BAD PEOPLE TO SURVIVE AND THRIVE AT THE WORKPLACE.

### UNDERESTIMATION

Good people underestimate how deep bad behavior is entrenched in an individual's persona.

For example, if a person takes office stationery home, would you categorize him as a bad person?

Krista Wolfe[2] shares that employee theft costs small US businesses about $40 billion every year. Rene Chun[3] says, "The Association of Certified Fraud Examiners reports that theft of 'non-cash' property — ranging from a single pencil in the supply closet to a pallet of them on the company loading dock — jumped from 10.6% of corporate theft losses in 2002 to 21% in 2018."

Yannick Griep[4] proposes that employees steal as an act of self-righteous vengeance. When the employer breaks a psychological contract[5], the employee settles the score by claiming his rightful due.

While this may be true part of the time, corporate theft is an indicator of character. The persons may be capable of greater damage to the organization if the opportunity presents itself. Organizations rarely flag the behavior and organizations with zero tolerance for theft are the exception.

## COGNITIVE DISSONANCE

*Cognitive dissonance*[6]

Good people discount the scope and scale of bad behavior. They do not believe anyone could be capable of being *so* bad.

When Captain Witold Pilecki[7] sneaked into Auschwitz[8] and reported the horrific activities to the outside world, the people who could have helped destroy Auschwitz thought that Pilecki was exaggerating about the scale of atrocities. If you missed the back story on Captain Witold Pilecki, read it here[9].

When you report colleagues who sabotage your efforts, cognitive dissonance may cause it to backfire on you. *You* may be labeled as unprofessional and a poor team player.

## DELUSION

Good people convince themselves that bad behavior won't continue or manifest in other forms. The delusion helps to avoid facing uncomfortable truths and making inconvenient choices.

For example, a salesperson has turned an under-performing territory to a profitable territory. As per the psychological contract in his mind, he deserves to continue growing the same territory and reap the benefits. You allocate a new territory to him. As a manager, you see this as a logical utilization of his talent. The sales person resents being weaned away and sabotages the efforts of the new salesperson. You think his behavior is transient. Eventually, he mines company data and joins the competitor.

## HANDICAPPED BY GOODNESS

Good people have mental limits that prevent understanding a bad person's modus operandi. It takes a bad person to know a bad person.

Frank Abagnale[10] is a security consultant who helps plug security gaps in banking infrastructure. He was a con man, check forger and imposter from the age of 15 up to 21 years old. Abagnale's story inspired the Academy Award nominated movie Catch Me If You Can (2002). In 1974, after he had served seven years of his twelve-year sentence, the United States federal government released him on the condition that he help the federal authorities to investigate crimes committed by fraud and scam artists. In 2015, Abagnale was named AARP Fraud Watch Ambassador[11], where he educates consumers on protecting themselves from identity theft and cyber crime. In 2018, he began co-hosting The Perfect Scam podcast[12] about how scammers operate.

## EMPATHY

Good persons may have empathy for the family or dependents associated with the bad person.

This happens when the employee is not 'bad' in the strict sense of the word. Rather, he underperforms consistently and drags the rest of the team down. The tolerance for underperformance fosters complacent behavior and makes matters worse. The team wonders why he is being given a long rope.

## HOPE

Good people hope that the bad person will outgrow bad behavior with guidance and mentorship.

This happens when the bad person is a close relation of someone in senior management. It is possible he was hired to be moulded and kept out of trouble. The personal agenda is frequently at the cost of team morale. However, nepotism[13] and cronyism[14] are a reality, and the little masters must be endured more often than not. If you step into the other person's shoes, your choices may not be different.

Having said that, the prudent CEO takes a decisive approach to curbing the effects of nepotism and cronyism. It is an ongoing process. Senior employees bring family and friends on board. Employees who work with friends are productive and happier. However, the balance sometimes tilts on the side of grayscale behavior, misaligned interests and white collar crime. Naresh Khatri and Eric W. K. Tsang[15] say, *"Crony capitalism, the granting of economic favors to friends and privileged associates is widely regarded as a key factor contributing to the Asian financial crisis of 1997[16]"*.

## IT IS A MATTER OF TIME

Every organization has corporate snakes-in-suits that are closely managed, defanged and let go. These individuals are self-serving at the cost of others and the organization. His character is not hidden from those at the top. He is on his way out, it's a matter of time.

## SELECTIVE BADNESS

The individual behaves badly with specific persons in specific situations. He has earned many brownie points for creating value. This offsets his behavior and grants benefit of doubt. It is a myopic approach to talent management.

## CULTURE

In certain cultures, bad behavior has a higher tolerance threshold. Employees from these cultures may require sensitivity training and a focused review of the organizational code of conduct.

Cultural alignment is a challenge when embracing diversity at the workplace. Few HR professionals are competent in leading difficult conversations associated with diversity. Regardless of the organizational code of conduct, sensitivity training and rules of etiquette, individuals will swing towards culture-driven default behavior. This is where they feel comfortable and truly themselves.

Tim Pile highlights culture-driven behavior in the blog article 'Who are the World's Worst Tourists?'[17] It brings a smile but not if it happened at the workplace.

## DESENSITIZATION

Good people are getting desensitized to bad behavior. Trolling and aggressive communication on social media are increasingly tolerated. People insult and attack one another because they are not face to face. When the same behavior crops up at the workplace, it is viewed with detachment, as if it were happening on social media.

Dana Wilkie[18] says, "If you have spent any time on social media, you will observe a degree of uncivil discourse that is brutal. Name calling, insulting, even threatening language have become the norm. This not only sets a low bar, but it normalizes harsh, aggressive communication. That comes to work."

## COST AS A BARRIER

The HR department argues that replacing a bad person does not guarantee a good person will take his place. They see the cost of repeated recruitment and departmental disruption as a barrier. It is the psychology of attachment to a poor decision because of the investments already made.

At other times, performance and behavior are not viewed separately. Bridget Miller[19] says, "Sometimes an employee is performing well and meeting job requirements, but behaves in ways that are disruptive."

## DEALING WITH BAD PEOPLE

Do not be fazed by bad people. Expect them to be at the workplace. Assess how 'bad' is the situation and decide if you can live with it on a day-to-day basis.

The preceding chapters delve into how bad people affect us and how to navigate the situations they create.

Bad people drain your energy quickly. Your first defense is to keep yourself recharged.

If both your home and workplace are abusive environments, carve a space for solitude, scrape a few moments of privacy to connect with higher energy. If you perish at the altar of burnout, bad people would cluck politely and say you couldn't cope with the competitive, fast-paced work culture.

## THE PSYCHOLOGICAL — THEOLOGICAL PERSPECTIVE

Author, Psychologist and Theologian Harold Ellens[20] says in the book 'Explaining Evil'[21], "The most profound evil lies not with pickpockets, streetwalkers, and drunks, nor with persons who are otherwise easily associated with troublesomeness. More significant evil should be sought among the well-dressed, the reputable, and especially the seemingly beneficent. This means that assessing good and evil requires a suspicious and penetrating mind. The most powerful and effective perpetrators of evil will take measures to assure that they have a beneficent public image. As Russell says — evil is grasped by the mind immediately and felt by the emotions; it is sensed as hurt deliberately inflicted. If we accept this elegantly simple reflection, we need not try to unpack definitions that would endlessly relativize evil, making one person's or culture's evil another person's or culture's good."

---

*Up next* ☞ *Heart Speak*

The meaning of your life.

# PART IV

# CHAPTER 20
# HEART SPEAK

*Each choice you make defines your future*
*To be motivated, not manipulated*
*To be useful, not used*
*Choose to listen to your inner voice, not the*
*    random opinions of others*
*Each choice you make defines your future*
*- Adapted from a quote attributed to Miranda*
*    Marrott*

This book is for you — The Intelligent Intern, The Noble Newbie, The Conscientious Manager, The Hands-On CEO. It is also for the employee with shades of grey. For what is dark except the absence of light?

## TO THE INTELLIGENT INTERN

Researchers claim the new generation is less smart[1] about assessing information. I say, you are not the new generation. You are you. Prove the stuffy old shirts[2] wrong.

## TO THE NOBLE NEWBIE

The workplace has a dual existence — you see one, the other exists outside your knowledge. Observe and look for unknown-unknowns.

## TO THE CONSCIENTIOUS MANAGER

Empirical evidence exists that employees lose hair in managerial positions. You manage the ones above, below and lateral to your place in the hierarchy. Inter-departmental cooperation and project management are often an exercise in yogic patience. Thank you for all you do.

## TO THE HANDS-ON CEO

Interns and newbies are the leaders of the future. Leave your legacy through their success and wisdom.

## TO THE GRAYSCALE EMPLOYEE

Noble traits are always in demand — everywhere. Even the mafia needs trustworthy and loyal persons within its inner circle. Utilize your sharp senses for more than a zero-sum game.

Sufistic wisdom describes the seven stages in the mastery of the *nafs*[3] — the self, psyche, ego.

*Nafs* is the lower self in its primitive stage. It deceives the self and others. No one is immune to it, not even religious leaders. Rumi[4] describes the *nafs* in religious hypocrisy, saying *"the nafs has a rosary[5] in its right hand, and a dagger in the slee*ve."

In the next stage, the *nafs* looks inward, conscience is awakened and man repents. Here the *nafs* is inspired by one's heart, it sees the results of one's actions, agrees with one's brain, acknowledges one's weaknesses, and aspires to perfection.

The next stage is *nafs* in inspired action. It seeks to build an inventory of good actions and liquidate the inventory of wrongdoing.

Next is the *nafs* at peace. It leaves bad manners behind, the soul is tranquil and life acquires meaning.

In the following stage, the *nafs* accepts cosmic wisdom and lives fully in the moment.

This is followed by a *nafs* that is forgiving and tolerant.

And finally, the *nafs* transforms to The Perfected Being, Al-Insān al-Kāmil[6], Narottam[7].

You are on a journey. Move through the stages.

A descriptive word for the heart in Arabic is *Qalb*[8] — it means that which alternates suddenly from one state to another. Oskar Schindler[9][10][11], St. Moses the Black[12][13], General Butt Naked[14][15], Nathan Bedford Forrest[16][17], Angulimala[18][19], Frank Abagnale[20], M.E. Thomas abruptly shifted from gray shadows towards light. Reflect upon their life stories.

The family as a source of values and guidance has ceased to exist. *You* are your own teacher and disciple. Regardless of the lessons you teach yourself, learn these lessons from a position of power. Gather the tools. Not for survival or transactional advantage, but to lead others.

Each choice you make defines your future. The future starts with defining the meaning of your life.

> 66 Ultimately, man should not ask what the meaning of his life is, but rather he must recognize that it is *he* who has been asked. In a word, each man is questioned by life; and he can only answer to life by answering for his own life; to life he can

only respond by being responsible[21]. ~ Viktor Frankl, Man's Search for Meaning, p. 131

Go on then, create *your* meaning of life.

*Up next* ☛ *Quotes for the Initiated*

The Initiated is the one who knows the truth.

# CHAPTER 21
# QUOTES FOR THE INITIATED

# QUOTES FOR THE INITIATED

The true meaning of life is to plant trees, under whose shade you do not plan to sit.

Nelson Henderson

If my life is going to mean anything, I have to live it myself.

Rick Riorda

The story you tell yourself is largely the story you are living.

Terence McKenna

If you don't give yourself permission to create a new world, chances are nobody else will.

James Altucher

Not everything that is faced can be changed. But nothing can be changed until it is faced.

James Baldwin

# CHAPTER 22
# WHY I WROTE THIS BOOK

The youngest CEO in the world is getting younger.

Hillary Yip was the youngest CEO in 2019-2020. She says, "My journey began almost five years ago at the age of ten when I ran into a child entrepreneurship contest and was intrigued. We had to create an idea with which we could change the world."

Hillary Yip on Entrepreneurship[1] 👇

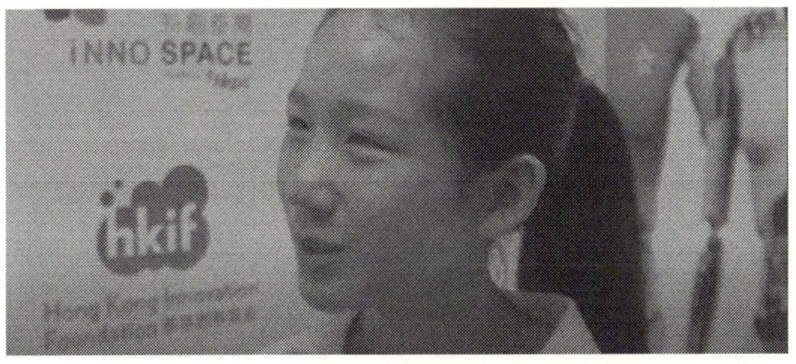


*Hillary Yip — the youngest CEO in the world —*
*2019 - 2020*

Suhas Gopinath[2] took charge of Globals Inc. as CEO at age 17 - three years after founding the company. At the time, he was the world's youngest CEO.

Hillary Yip and Suhas Gopinath chose to be the CEO. But if they hadn't, would CEO habits wither up and die? The answer is no, of course. You don't need to be a CEO to build CEO habits. Managers, newbies and interns nurture CEO habits to excel in their roles.

Cut to the HR professionals. They peruse thousands of resumes and conduct hundreds of recruitment interviews. Candidates still offer unoriginal, outdated responses to interview questions. The quest for an exceptional candidate bites the dust more often than not.

Companies must hire to meet strategic objectives and timelines. I figured, why not enjoy the process? So I meet candidates in informal settings, share stories & laughter, and hire on the premise of building the next generation of leaders.

I won't do it for long; hence this book. The CEO habits and 12th non-habit described here pack sufficient dynamite to take you from where you are to where you want to be.

CEO habits are hidden in plain sight. Observe the individuals who live these habits. Stand on the shoulders of giants. Then be a giant and build a legacy.

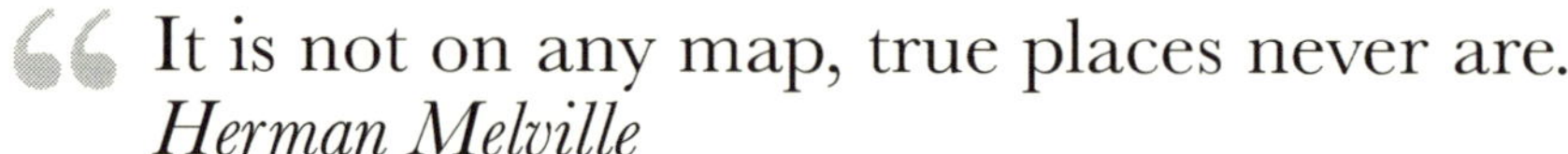 It is not on any map, true places never are.
*Herman Melville*

SUKHDEEP
SACHDEV
about the author
You didn't come this far to only come this far.
Get going.

*"A CEO has time to write a book?" "Nah!"*

Sukhdeep Sachdev is the Global Chief Executive Officer of a distribution network serving education, life sciences and medical technology verticals. The business comprises 11 companies across MENA, APAC and North America regions. His insights leverage three decades of stakeholder relationships in diversity-centric business environments. He travels extensively, and connects with hundreds of CEOs committed to innovation, excellence and well-being. He is a subject matter expert in portfolio management, value-based strategy, and integrative leadership.

amazon.com/author/sukhdeepsachdev

linkedin.com/in/sukhdeepsachdev

# CREDITS

An acknowledgment of thanks to the websites and artists that provided base graphics for the composite illustrations in the book ☞

*You are my family, but you know it not.*

*You are my companion*

*Across the timeless stretch of creative tasks*

*In the solitary hours of the mornings*

*In the calm dusk of the evenings*

*Day in and day out*

*You are my family, but you know it not.*

— Shabnam Mohammad Ateeq Ansari[1], Illustrator, 11 CEO Habits.

## VECTORS AND IMAGES

Pixabay[2], Public Domain Vectors[3], Freepik[4], Seekpng[5], FlyClipArt[6], Pngwing[7], Favpng[8], Clipartmax[9], Clipart-Library[10], PNGkey[11], DLpng[12], ClipartKey[13], WebstockReview[14], PNGio[15], WPclipart[16], NicePNG[17], Vecteezy[18]

## VECTORIZER TOOL

Rapid Resizer[19]

## PNG COMPRESSION

Website Planet[20]

## FONTS

Font Squirrel[21], Font Space[22]

## ILLUSTRATION DESIGN TOOL

Inkscape[23]

## BOOK DESIGN TOOL

Vellum[24]

## EDITING AND COPY MANAGEMENT TOOL

ProWritingAid[25]

## BOOK MOCKUP TOOL

Mockup Shots[26]

# THE READING LIST

## *AFFILIATE DISCLOSURE*

*The links are affiliated to the Amazon Associates program. This means that publishers make a commission if you use the links. This is at no cost to you.*

*Use ISBN Search if you don't want to use affiliate links. ISBNs appear below and in the endnote of respective chapters.*

## CHAPTER 3 - WINNING WITH WORDS

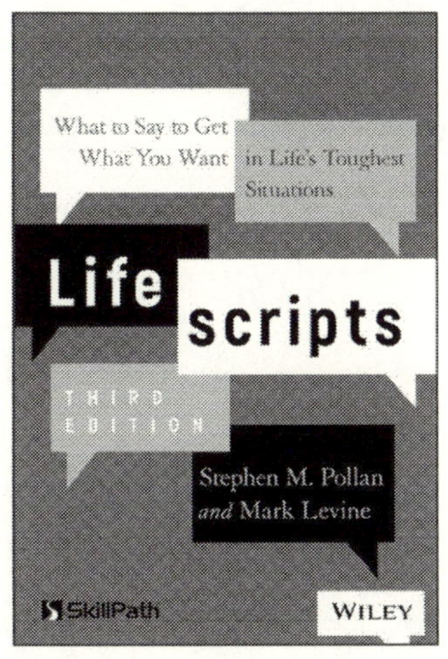


**Lifescripts: What to say to get what you want in life's toughest situations.** *Stephen M. Pollan and Mark Levine. ISBN — 978— 1119571971, 978—0— 471— 63101— 9*

Lifescripts [1] — https://amzn.to/2GfoTqJ (this is an affiliate link)

**Workscripts: Perfect Phrases for High-Stakes Conversations.** *Stephen M. Pollan and Mark Levine. ISBN —978— 0— 470— 63324— 3*

Workscripts[2] — https://amzn.to/35UdlSr (this is an affiliate link)

**Exactly What To Say — The Magic Words For Influence And Impact.** *By Phil M Jones. ISBN: 978— 0— 692— 88195— 8 (paperback) ISBN: 978— 0— 692— 88196 — 5 (eBook)*

Exactly What To Say[3] — https://amzn.to/31Zz2zA (this is an affiliate link)

**How To Win Any Argument — Without Raising Your Voice, Losing Your Cool, Or Coming To Blows.** *By Robert Mayer ISBN: 978— 1601631817*

How To Win Any Argument[4] — https://amzn.to/3jKFIrl (this is an affiliate link)

# CHAPTER 6 - LEARNING BY OBSERVATION

**Sensation & Perception**. *10th Edition. By E. Bruce Goldstein, James Brockmole. ISBN: 978— 1305580299*

Sensation & Perception[5] — https://amzn.to/35Sxk3U (this is an affiliate link)

# CHAPTER 8 - SITUATIONAL AWARENESS

**Sleights of Mind.** *By Stephen L. Macknik and Susana Martinez-Conde ISBN: 978-0312611675*

Sleights of Mind[6] — https://amzn.to/3oGAiBb (this is an affiliate link)

**Spy Secrets That Can Save Your Life: A Former CIA Officer Reveals Safety and Survival Techniques to Keep You and Your Family Protected.** *By Jason Hanson. ISBN: 978-0399175671*

Spy Secrets That Can Save Your Life[7] — https://amzn.to/380Q1VH (this is an affiliate link)

**What Every BODY Is Saying — An ex-FBI agent's guide to speed reading people.** *By Joe Navarro with Marvin Karlins. ISBN: 978— 0— 06— 164486— 3*

What Every BODY Is Saying[8] — https://amzn.to/35OoPqx (this is an affiliate link)

---

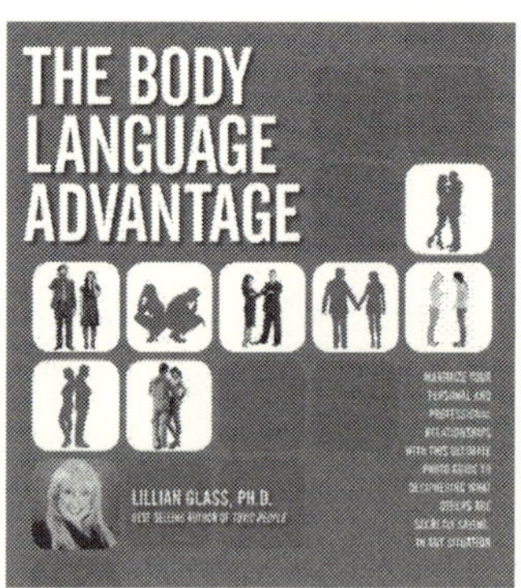

**The Body Language Advantage — Maximize your personal and professional relationships with this ultimate photo guide to deciphering what others are secretly saying, in any situation.** *By Lillian Glass.*

*ISBN: 978— 1— 59233— 515— 2 eISBN: 978— 1— 61058— 407— 4*

The Body Language Advantage[9] — https://amzn.to/35OolRf (this is an affiliate link)

**Body Language — Learn how to read others and communicate with confidence.** *By Elizabeth Kuhnke. ISBN: 9780857087041 (print), 9780857087034*

Body Language[10] — https://amzn.to/37WE1EM (this is an affiliate link)

**The Silent Language Of Leaders — How body language can help or hurt how you lead.** *By Carol Kinsey Goman. ISBN: 978— 0— 470— 87636— 7*

The Silent Language Of Leaders[11] — https://amzn.to/34JFEDW (this is an affiliate link)

---

**Reading People — How to understand people and predict their behavior, anytime, anyplace.** *By Jo-Ellan Dimitrius and Mark Mazzarella. ISBN: 978— 0— 345— 50413— 5*

Reading People[12] — https://amzn.to/31VsQZa (this is an affiliate link)

**The Definitive Book of Body Language — The hidden meaning behind people's gestures and expressions.** *By Allan & Barbara Pease. ISBN: 978— 0553804720*

The Definitive Book of Body Language[13] — https://amzn.to/3mD4uv3 (this is an affiliate link)

**I Can Read You Like A Book — How to spot the messages and emotions people are really sending with their body language.** *By Gregory Hartley and Maryann Karinch. ISBN: 978— 156414— 941— 1*

I Can Read You Like A Book[14] — https://amzn.to/ 3oDvooF (this is an affiliate link)

**You Say More Than You Think — A 7-day plan for using the new body language to get what you want.** *By Janine Driver with Mariska van Aalst. eISBN: 978— 0— 307 — 45399— 0[15]*

You Say More Than You Think — https://amzn.to/ 2Jo25pX (this is an affiliate link)

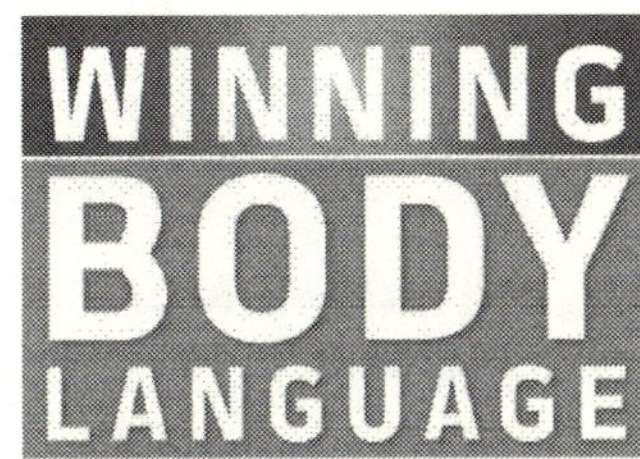

**Winning Body Language — Control the conversation, command attention and convey the right message — without saying a word.** *By Mark Bowden. ISBN: 978— 0— 07— 170164— 8*

[16]Winning Body Language — https://amzn.to/2HGJ2Xx (this is an affiliate link)

**Without Saying A Word — Master the science of body language & maximize your success.** *By Kasia Wezowski and Patrick Wezowski. ISBN: 978— 0— 8144— 3974— 6 (eBook)*

Without Saying A Word[17] — https://amzn.to/37WATZy (this is an affiliate link)

# CHAPTER 9 - EXECUTIVE PRESENCE

**Executive Presence: The Missing Link Between Merit and Success.** *By Sylvia Ann Hewlett ISBN: 978-0062246899*

Executive Presence[18] — https://amzn.to/320rz2U (this is an affiliate link)

**Real Leaders Don't Do PowerPoint: How to Sell Yourself and Your Ideas.** *By Christopher Witt and Dale Fetherling. ISBN: 978-0307407702*

Real Leaders Don't Do Powerpoint[19] — https://amzn.to/381wkNK (this is an affiliate link)

**Never Split The Difference — Negotiating as if your life depended on it.** *By Chris Voss with Tahl Raz*
*ISBN: 978— 0— 06— 240780— 1*

Never Split The Difference[20] — https://amzn.to/2TI8DBH (this is an affiliate link)

**Negotiation Genius — How to overcome obstacles and achieve brilliant results at the bargaining table and beyond.** *By Deepak Malhotra and Max H. Bazerman. eISBN: 978— 0— 55390494— 9*

Negotiation Genius[21] — https://amzn.to/3oIY8fH (this is an affiliate link)

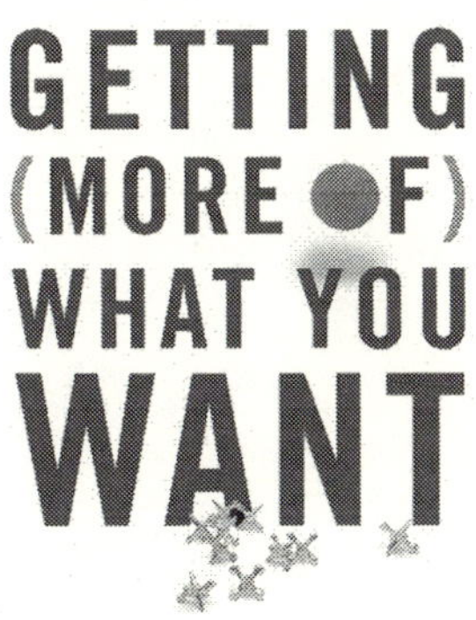

**Getting (More Of) What You Want — How the secrets of economics and psychology can help you negotiate anything, in business and life.** *By Margaret A. Neale and Thomas Z. Lys ISBN: 978— 0— 465— 05072— 7 (hardcover) ISBN: 978— 0— 465— 04063— 6 (eBook)*

Getting (More Of) What You Want[22] — https://amzn.to/37YkPq8 (this is an affiliate link)



**Getting To Yes — Negotiating agreement without giving in.** *2nd Edition. By Roger Fisher, William Try and Bruce Patton. ISBN: 978— 0— 14— 015735— 2*

Getting To Yes[23] — https://amzn.to/3mFb8ku (this is an affiliate link)

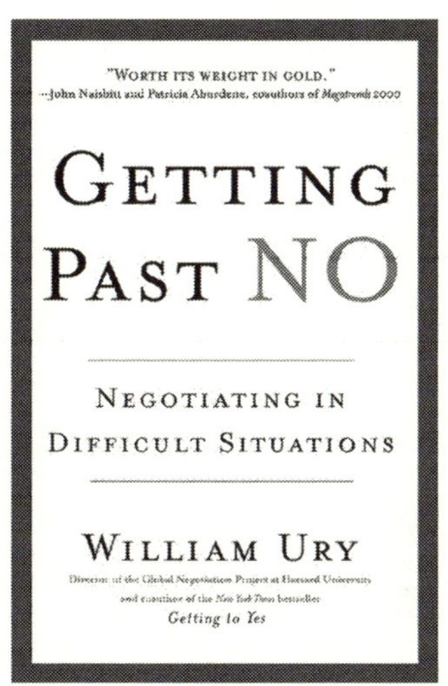

**Getting Past No — Negotiating in difficult situations.** *By William Try. eISBN: 978— 0— 55390364— 5*

Getting Past No[24] — https://amzn.to/2JpfWfF (this is an affiliate link)

# CHAPTER 11 - ATTENTION TO DETAIL

**The Power Of Noticing — What the best leaders see.** *By Max H. Bazerman. ISBN: 978— 1— 4767— 0029— 8 (print book) ISBN: 978— 1— 47670031— 1 (eBook)*

The Power Of Noticing[25] — https://amzn.to/3jKyeEL (this is an affiliate link)

---

**Can I Have Your Attention — How to think fast, find your focus and sharpen your concentration.** *By Joseph Cardillo. ISBN: 978— 1— 60163— 063— 6*

Can I Have Your Attention[26] — https://amzn.to/ 2HU8RTP (this is an affiliate link)

**The Sheikh CEO — Lessons in leadership from Mohammed Bin Rashid Al Maktoum.** *By Dr. Yasar Jarrar ISBN: 978— 1— 78596— 110— 6*

The Sheikh CEO[27] — https://amzn.to/3kLdRsh (this is an affiliate link)

**Everything Is F*cked: A Book about Hope.** *By Mark Manson. ISBN: 978— 0062888433*

Everything Is F*cked[28] — https://amzn.to/3kJkLhL (this is an affiliate link)

## CHAPTER 13 - THE 12TH NON-HABIT

**Please don't just do what I tell you! Do what needs to be done.** *By Bob Nelson. ISBN: 978-0786867295*

Please Don't Just Do What I Tell You! Do What Needs To Be Done.[29] — https://amzn.to/2I8BpJx (this is an affiliate link)

*This eBook is for the use of anyone, anywhere, at no cost, and with almost no restrictions whatsoever. You may copy it, give it away, or re-use it under the terms of the Project Gutenberg License included with this eBook.*

## THE PROJECT GUTENBERG EBOOK OF A MESSAGE TO GARCIA, BY ELBERT HUBBARD[30]

### Direct download link

*No sign-in or email address required*

https://book.11ceohabits.com/bookfunnelgarcia

**3:59.4: The Quest to Break the 4 Minute Mile.** *By John Bryant. ISBN: 978— 0099469087*

3:59.4[31] — https://amzn.to/3oKCeJ2 (this is an affiliate link)

# CHAPTER 17 - THE GRAYSCALE EMPLOYEE

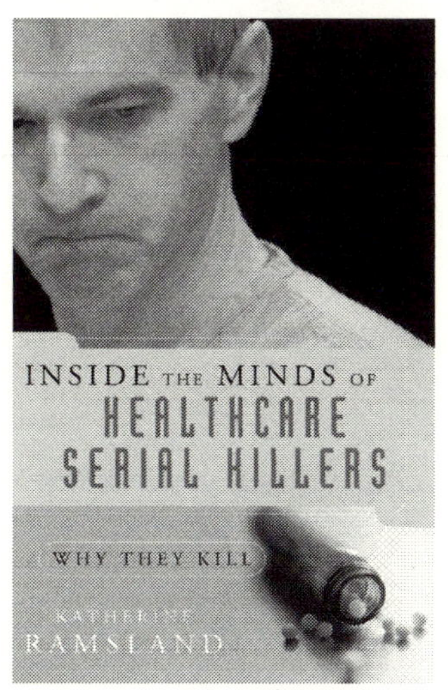

**Inside The Minds Of Healthcare Serial Killers —
Why they kill.** *By Katherine Ramsland ISBN: 978— 0— 275
— 99422— 8*

Inside The Minds Of Healthcare Serial Killers[32] —
https://amzn.to/3jKmSAn (this is an affiliate link)

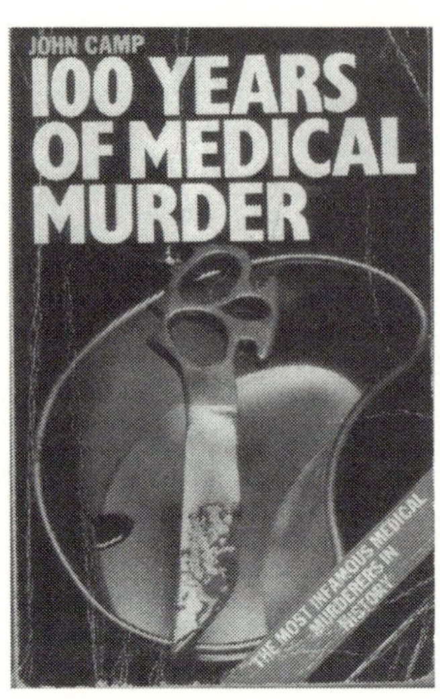

**One Hundred Years Of Medical Murder.** *By John Camp ISBN: 978— 0586056172*

One Hundred Years Of Medical Murder[33] — https://amzn.to/2TC9bZT (this is an affiliate link)

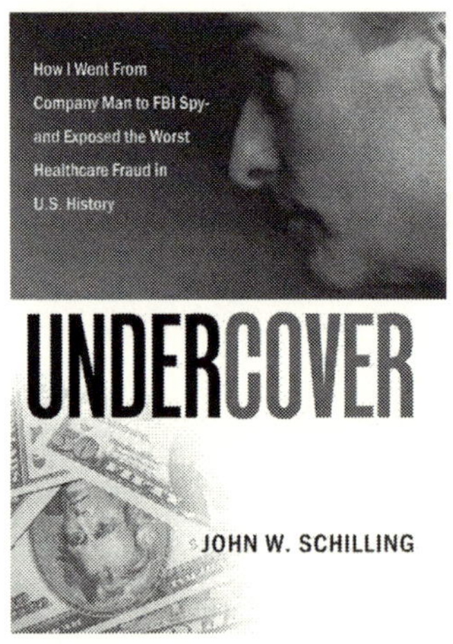


**Undercover — How I went from company man to FBI spy and exposed the worst healthcare fraud in**

**US history.** *By John W. Schilling. ISBN: 978— 1452055084 Undercover*[34] — https://amzn.to/3eb5oMx (this is an affiliate link)

# CHAPTER 18 - PERSONAL POWER

**Secrets to Winning at Office Politics: How to Achieve Your Goals and Increase Your Influence at Work.** *By Marie G. McIntyre ISBN: 978-0312332181*

Secrets to Winning at Office Politics[35] — https://amzn.to/2TWuDch (this is an affiliate link)

**Confessions of a Sociopath: A Life Spent Hiding in Plain Sight.** *By M.E. Thomas. ISBN: 978-0307956651*

Confessions of a Sociopath[36] — https://amzn.to/ 34OotB9 (this is an affiliate link)

---

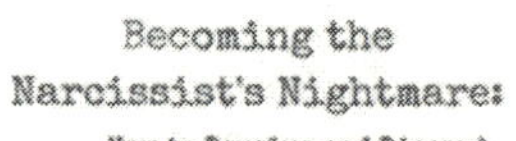

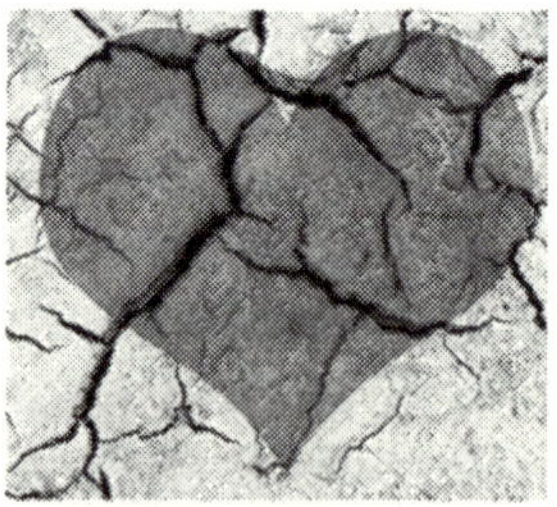


**Becoming the Narcissist's Nightmare: How to Devalue and Discard the Narcissist While**

**Supplying yourself.** *By Shahida Arabi. ISBN: 978-1523702466*

Becoming the Narcissist's Nightmare[37] — https://amzn.to/3oNTYDd (this is an affiliate link)

---

**Explaining Evil.** *By J. Harold Ellens. ISBN: 978-0313387159*

Explaining Evil[38] — https://amzn.to/2TMY9km (this is an affiliate link)

Here is the link to leave a review on Amazon

11 CEO Habits[39] — https://amzn.to/326yyay (this is an affiliate link)

11 CEO Habits - Wake Up The CEO Within You: The Ultimate Guide For Managers, Newbies And Interns. By Sukhdeep Sachdev. ISBN: 978— *1*— *7357986*— *7*— *7*

Broken links in the book? Drop me a line.

mail@11ceohabits.com

# THE BLOG LIST

## CHAPTER 3 - WINNING WITH WORDS

A Man's Word Is His Bond — 4 Tips To Keep Your Promises[1]

How to Write an Elevator Pitch[2]

7 Comebacks to a Verbal Bully[3]

Top Ten Clean Comebacks and Roasts[4]

Top Ten Counter Comebacks to Other People's Comebacks[5]

25 Funny Ways to Say NO[6]

## CHAPTER 5 - CLARITY OF THOUGHT AND SPEECH

Clear Communication is About Structure[7]

## CHAPTER 7 - SPEED OF FOLLOW-THROUGH

Speed as a Habit[8]

## CHAPTER 17 - THE GRAYSCALE EMPLOYEE

Dealing with Energy-Sucking 'Deadwood' Employees[9]

# THE VIDEO LIST

## CHAPTER 11 - ATTENTION TO DETAIL

Change Blindness[1]

The Monkey Business Illusion[2]

The 3 Types Of Attention to Detail[3]

## CHAPTER 14 - THE SECRET KPIS

The Miracle Worker — Helen's First Lesson[4]

## CHAPTER 20 - HEART SPEAK

Hillary Yip on Entrepreneurship[5]

# THE DOWNLOAD LIST

*This eBook is for the use of anyone, anywhere, at no cost, and with almost no restrictions whatsoever. You may copy it, give it away, or re-use it under the terms of the Project Gutenberg License included with this eBook.*

**THE PROJECT GUTENBERG EBOOK OF A MESSAGE TO GARCIA, BY ELBERT HUBBARD** [1]

**Direct download link** *No sign-in or email address required*

https://book.11ceohabits.com/bookfunnelgarcia

# LINKS & REFERENCES

## 1. CEO HABITS - HIDDEN IN PLAIN SIGHT

1.  The manager is in the middle of the organizational hierarchy. She is criticized both ways — when she **behaves** like a manager and when she **doesn't behave** like a manager.

    The manager was once a star salesperson or a one-man team — achieving targets and working alone. As a manager, he follows orders *and* gives orders, meets targets *and* assigns targets, works alone *and* with others. She has new KPIs — inspire the team, drive results through others, build a personal brand. It is a tough balancing act.
2.  Newbie — The employee on a full-time job for the first time.
3.  Interns are students who work in a company for university credits and exposure to workplace culture.
4.  Penalize — To put at an unfair disadvantage
5.  Sit on the fence — Not sure which choice is better.
6.  Toe the line — To do as expected without causing 'trouble' for anyone
7.  Disruptive — Innovative or groundbreaking
8.  Trait — a distinguishing characteristic or quality, especially of one's personal nature.

## 2. STANDING ON THE SHOULDERS OF GIANTS

1.  A cheat sheet is a set of notes used for quick reference. Cheat sheets are so named because students use them without the instructor's knowledge to cheat on a test.
2.  Dupe means to deceive or trick.
3.  'To be swamped' means to be burdened or overwhelmed with something.
4.  'To self-destruct' means to destroy the self by collapsing, exploding or disintegrating automatically.

5. Teaching someone to fish means teaching how to do something. It is more helpful to them in the long run than just doing it for them.
6. **OMG** is an abbreviation of the expression **oh my God** (or oh my goodness or oh my gosh) and in the domain of text and instant messaging, social media etc, has become a popular mechanism for expressing surprise or astonishment
7. The learning curve theory is a way to understand the performance improvement of an employee. The idea is, the more an employee does something, the better they will get at it.
8. The comfort zone is a situation where one feels safe or at ease. It is a settled method of working that requires little effort and yields only barely acceptable results.
9. **Sales Force Automation** (SFA) refers to software apps for sales management. SFA provides automated workflows that create a streamlined sales process to manage business leads, sales forecast, and team performance.
10. Talent development focuses on how to develop employee skills and competencies. Organizations provide learning opportunities and tools for employees to advance their overall careers. Talent development is a business strategy that companies implement to retain talented employees. https://book.11ceohabits.com/talentdevelopment
11. **Brownie points** in modern usage are an imaginary social currency, gained by doing good deeds or earning favor in the eyes of another, often one's superior.
12. Delusion is an unshakable belief in something untrue.
13. Hierarchy is a system in which employees are ranked according to relative status, seniority or authority.
14. **Curate** means to select and organize something for the convenience of the user.
15. A **Rolodex** is a rotating file device used to store business contact information.
16. Customer relationship management (CRM) is a technology for managing relationships and interactions with customers and potential customers. When people say CRM, they are usually referring to a CRM system, a tool that helps with contact management, sales management, agent productivity, and more. https://book.11ceohabits.com/crm
17. Bitrix24 is a software service developed by Bitrix, Inc. providing a company with a full range of team collaboration and social networking tools. The service is for small and mid-scale businesses. An end user can choose between the free and paid

licenses depending on the number of employees and features required. https://book.11ceohabits.com/bitrix24

18. Hashtag is a word or phrase preceded by a hash sign (#), used on social media websites and applications, especially Twitter, to identify messages on a specific topic. They make it easier to discover posts around those specific topics, because hashtags aggregate all social media content with that same hashtag. Adding hashtags increases the visibility of a post, and it is easy to overdo it.

19. Email personalization is an email marketing process that uses personal information to produce targeted emails. It gives individual treatment to the customer and increases email marketing results. "When you want to squeeze juice from an orange, half of it can go to trash, because you didn't try hard enough. Email personalization is an approach that helps you squeeze your orange to the last drop". https://book.11ceohabits.com/email

20. Document management is a system or process used to produce, capture, track and store electronic documents such as PDFs, word processing files and digital images of paper-based content.

21. **Tactics** are the action taken to support business strategy.

22. The concept of situational power indicates that a person very low down the food chain can have absolute power in certain situations, overriding those who are much higher in the hierarchy. For instance, a bouncer could refuse entrance when approached by a top hotshot. https://book.11ceohabits.com/situationalpower

23. A subject matter expert is an individual with a deep understanding of a particular job, process, department, function, technology, machine, material or type of equipment. Individuals designated as subject matter experts are typically sought out by others interested in leveraging their unique expertise to solve specific problems or help meet challenges. https://book.11ceohabits.com/subjectmatterexpert

24. Role models show young people how to live with integrity, optimism, hope, determination, and compassion. Wikipedia defines it as a person whose behavior, example, or success is or can be emulated by others, especially by younger people. The term *role model* is credited to sociologist Robert K. Merton. https://book.11ceohabits.com/rolemodel and https://book.11ceohabits.com/robertmerton

25. A value framework is a model that establishes how value is created for self and others, and the strategy to manage returns derived from that value.
26. The personal development roadmap is a route plan of the goals and successes you plan to achieve and the skills and habits you'll need to achieve them.
27. A mentor is a colleague, supervisor, or friend who guides a less experienced person by building trust and modeling positive behaviors. Mentors are an important part of personal and professional development. At the core of the relationship, a mentor is available to their mentee to offer advice, provide support and answer questions. The mentor may be older or younger than the person being mentored, but they must have a certain area of expertise. https://book.11ceohabits.com/mentorship
28. The devil's advocate is a person who **advocates** an opposing approach to provoke debate, to expose it to a thorough examination or test the strength of the opposing arguments.
29. A **murder board** is an arranged exercise designed to expose risks in a future project, event or idea. It is a panel of individuals, usually executives of senior managers, who review projects at different stages to determine whether the project should continue. The term originated in the US military, specifically from the Pentagon, but is also used in academic and government appointment contexts. https://book.11ceohabits.com/murderboard

# 3. WINNING WITH WORDS

1. A Gentleman's word is binding because what is said has value, and actions must follow. A bond is something you are obligated to fulfill. For instance, if you tell a friend that you will be at their house at 5 p.m. and don't show up, you have demonstrated your words do not have any value. https://book.11ceohabits.com/gentlemansword
2. An elevator pitch is a brief, persuasive speech that you use to spark interest in what your organization does. You can also use them to create interest in a project, idea, or product — or in yourself. A good elevator pitch should last no longer than a quick elevator ride of 20 to 30 seconds, hence the name. https://book.11ceohabits.com/elevatorpitch

3.  A comeback is a quick, witty reply. If someone insults you, and you say something back that turns the insult around, that's a comeback. https://book.11ceohabits.com/comeback

4.  Lifescripts: What to say to get what you want in life's toughest situations. Stephen M. Pollan and Mark Levine. ISBN — 978 — 1119571971, 0— 471— 63101— 9 (trade edition), 0— 471— 64376— 9 (special edition with CD).

5.  Antonio Centeno is the founder of the blog Real Men, Real Style https://book.11ceohabits.com/realmenrealstyle

6.  Link to the blog article A Man's Word Is His Bond — 4 Tips To Keep Your Promises http://book.11ceohabits.com/promises

7.  Michael Tomaszewski is a Certified Professional Resume Writer and founder of the blog Zety zety.com

8.  Link to blog article How to Write an Elevator Pitch https://book.11ceohabits.com/zetypitch

9.  Dr. Mark Goulston is a contributing writer to The Business Journals https://book.11ceohabits.com/bizjournals

10. Link to blog article 7 Comebacks to a Verbal Bully https://book.11ceohabits.com/verbalbully

11. Top Ten Clean Comebacks and Roasts https://book.11ceohabits.com/cleancomebacks

12. Top ten counter comebacks to other people's comebacks https://book.11ceohabits.com/replytocomebacks

13. 25 Funny Ways to Say NO https://book.11ceohabits.com/funnyno

14. Lifescripts: What to say to get what you want in life's toughest situations. Stephen M. Pollan and Mark Levine. ISBN — 978 — 1119571971, 0— 471— 63101— 9 (trade edition), 0— 471— 64376— 9 (special edition with CD).

15. Lifescripts on the Internet Archive — Reading time limit is 1 hour.

16. Internet Archive is a non— profit digital library offering free universal access to books, movies, software, music, podcasts, websites and more. archive.org

17. Order the print edition of Lifescripts, not the ebook. The script algorithm is easier to view in the print book.

18. Jill Lightner is a Seattle— based food writer. She is the author of 'Scraps, Peels and Stems: Recipes and Tips for Rethinking Food Waste at Home'. jilllightner.com

19. Exactly What To Say — The Magic Words For Influence And Impact. By Phil M Jones ISBN: 978— 0— 692— 88195 — 8 (paperback) ISBN: 978— 0— 692— 88196— 5 (eBook)

20.  How To Win Any Argument — Without Raising Your Voice, Losing Your Cool, Or Coming To Blows. By Robert Mayer ISBN: 978— 1601631817

## 4. BREVITY

1.  Harry Houdini was an illusionist and stunt performer noted for his escape acts. He freed himself from jails, handcuffs, chains, ropes, straitjackets, often while hanging from a rope in sight of street audiences.
2.  Hypothetical situation — Imaginary situation visualized for learning purposes.
3.  Do— or— die — used to describe a critical situation where one's actions may cause victory or defeat.
4.  Putting your foot in your mouth — unintentionally saying something that places you at a disadvantage.
5.  Pound of flesh — A pound of flesh was demanded as payment by moneylender Shylock from debtor Antonio in William Shakespeare's The Merchant of Venice. The human heart weighs a pound. In modern use, offering a pound of flesh means foregoing or giving away something precious to appease an injured party.

## 5. CLARITY OF THOUGHT AND SPEECH

1.  From GR8 Leaders blog article — Clear Communication is About Structure https://book.11ceohabits.com/communication
2.  The Here-There-Do sequence is inspired by The Gr8 Leaders Thought-Talk System®
3.  Winging it means you start speaking immediately and figure out the response along the way.
4.  Dysgraphia is a learning disability characterized by problems with writing. It's a neurological disorder that can affect children or adults. People with dysgraphia tend to use the wrong word for what they're trying to communicate. https://book.11ceohabits.com/dysgraphia
5.  Expressive language disorders involve deficits in verbal and written expression. Deficits may involve articulation, vocabu-

lary, sentence formation and memory. An adult's language ability will lag behind that of his/her peers in areas such as word choice and usage, sentence formation and grammar. https://book.11ceohabits.com/expressivelanguagedisorder

6.  Expressive Language Disorder makes it difficult for someone to express himself or make sense of what is being said to him. The individual struggles to produce language, speak in grammatically correct sentences, or translate thoughts into speech. The disorder can cause a person to misinterpret instructions, ignore when she's being spoken to, or take simple jokes too seriously.                                   https://book.11ceohabits.com/receptivelanguagedisorder

7.  Link to quote — Simmonds' clarity of thought, penetrating analyses and independence of spirit made him appear a strong character. *Cambridge Dictionary* https://book.11ceohabits.com/clarity

# 6. LEARNING BY OBSERVATION

1.  Elements — basic components.
2.  Concurrent — existing, happening, or done at the same time
3.  Raw data — bits of information that don't mean anything on their own. *For example, observing that Cathy is driving at a speed of 120 miles per hour means nothing unless it is also known that the speed limit on that road is 80 miles per hour.*
4.  Cognitive framework means the foundational intelligence to understand the larger picture and the context of the observation. *For example, the observation that Fred spilled tea on his suit is meaningful if he did it deliberately to escape a situation. If it is an accident, the meaningfulness of the observation is limited to managing the disruption.*
5.  Impediment — a hindrance or obstruction to doing something.
6.  Confirmation bias is the tendency to interpret new information as supporting one's existing beliefs and theories.
7.  Halo effect — when a positive impression generates highly favorable but inaccurate judgment of person, event, company, brand or product.
8.  Cognitive dissonance is a psychological adjustment to keep belief and action in harmony. *For example, a smoker convinces himself that smoking is not a big deal. Here, smoking is the action and*

*'not a big deal' is the belief — both are in harmony. To smoke and at the same time believe it is harmful creates mental discomfort. The mental discomfort is called cognitive dissonance. Hence, the smoker convinces himself that smoking is 'not a big deal'.*

9. Sensation & Perception, 10th Edition, *ISBN— 13*: 978—1305580299, *Authors*: E. Bruce Goldstein, James Brockmole

10. VARK Modalities — are Visual, Aural, Read/Write & Kinesthetic. Your VARK scores indicate how you prefer to learn. Preferences are influenced by natural disposition, life experiences, and workplace constraints. Learn more about it at https://book.11ceohabits.com/vark Test yourself for free at https://book.11ceohabits.com/varktest

11. Multiple Intelligences test — Test yourself for free at https://book.11ceohabits.com/multipleintelligences

# 7. SPEED OF FOLLOW-THROUGH

1. VUCA is the acronym for volatility, uncertainty, complexity, and ambiguity. To learn more What VUCA Really Means for You https://book.11ceohabits.com/vuca

2. Agile is a process involving constant collaboration with stakeholders and continuous improvement and iteration at every stage. To learn more, What is Agile Methodology in Project Management? https://book.11ceohabits.com/agile

3. Agility has four components: Results agility — achieves results under arduous conditions; has presence and competence to galvanize others to perform; Mental agility — deliberates difficult problems to discover solutions; comfortable with complexity and ambiguity; People agility — has extensive self — awareness; able to flex to diversity of conjectures and styles; resilient and constructive under pressure; Change agility — enjoys experimenting with novel conceptions; welcomes responsibility and unfamiliar challenges. Reference blog article Learning agility: Key to leading in a VUCA world. https://book.11ceohabits.com/agilityinvuca

4. Dave Girouard is the CEO of personal finance startup Upstart, and former President of Google Enterprise Apps. He is known for building Google's enterprise apps division into a $1B+ global business.

5. Link to blog article Speed as a Habit https://book.11ceohabits.com/speedhabit

6. Reference blog article Speed as a Habit https://book.11ceohabits.com/speedhabit
7. Antonio Centeno is the founder of the blog Real Men, Real Style https://book.11ceohabits.com/realmenrealstyle
8. Gary Vaynerchuk is the CEO of Vayner Media and acclaimed internet personality https://book.11ceohabits.com/garyvaynerchuk

# 8. SITUATIONAL AWARENESS

1. Sleights of Mind by Stephen L. Macknik and Susana Martinez-Conde ISBN: 978-0312611675
2. Speaker and magician Mac King shares an incident — is paraphrased from Chapter 8: Expectations and Assumption: How Magicians make ASSes of U and ME of the book Sleights of Mind by Stephen L. Macknik and Susana Martinez -Conde. ISBN: 978-0312611675
3. Jason Hanson is a former CIA Officer and the New York Times bestselling author of *Spy Secrets That Can Save Your Life.* As a security specialist, Hanson teaches anti-kidnapping, escape and evasion, evasive driving and much more. To learn more https://book.11ceohabits.com/spyescape
4. Spy Secrets That Can Save Your Life: A Former CIA Officer Reveals Safety and Survival Techniques to Keep You and Your Family Protected. By Jason Hanson. ISBN: 978-0399175671
5. Citation: Strater, Laura & Faulkner, L. & Hyatt, J. & Endsley, Mica. (2006). Supporting Situation Awareness Under Data Overload in Command and Control Visualizations. http://book.11ceohabits.com/dataoverload
6. Citation: Regis, Nicolas and Dehais, Frédéric and Rachelson, Emmanuel and Thooris, Charles and Pizziol, Sergio and Causse, Mickael and Tessier, Catherine Formal Detection of Attentional Tunneling in Human Operator— Automation Interactions. (2014) IEEE Transactions on Human— Machine Systems. pp. 1— 11. ISSN 2168— 2291 https://book.11ceohabits.com/attentiontunneling
7. Reference article Complexity Decreases Situation Awareness, Increases Human Error https://book.11ceohabits.com/requisitememorytrap
8. I Can Read You Like A Book — How to spot the messages and emotions people are really sending with their body lan-

guage. By Gregory Hartley and Maryann Karinch. ISBN: 978— 156414— 941— 1

You Say More Than You Think — A 7-day plan for using the new body language to get what you want. By Janine Driver with Mariska van Aalst. eISBN: 978— 0— 307— 45399— 0

Winning Body Language — Control the conversation, command attention and convey the right message — without saying a word. By Mark Bowden. ISBN: 978— 0— 07— 170164— 8

Without Saying A Word — Master the science of body language & maximize your success. By Kasia Wezowski and Patrick Wezowski. ISBN: 978— 0— 8144— 3974— 6 (eBook)

9. What Every BODY Is Saying — An ex-FBI agent's guide to speed reading people. By Joe Navarro with Marvin Karlins. ISBN: 978— 0— 06— 164486— 3

10. The Body Language Advantage — Maximize your personal and professional relationships with this ultimate photo guide to deciphering what others are secretly saying, in any situation. By Lillian Glass. ISBN: 978— 1— 59233— 515— 2 eISBN: 978— 1— 61058— 407— 4

11. Body Language — Learn how to read others and communicate with confidence. By Elizabeth Kuhnke. ISBN: 9780857087041 (print), 9780857087034

12. The Silent Language Of Leaders — How body language can help or hurt how you lead. By Carol Kinsey Goman. ISBN: 978— 0— 470— 87636— 7

13. Reading People — How to understand people and predict their behavior, anytime, anyplace. By Jo-Ellan Dimitrius and Mark Mazzarella. ISBN: 978— 0— 345— 50413— 5

14. The Definitive Book of Body Language — The hidden meaning behind people's gestures and expressions. By Allan & Barbara Pease. ISBN: 978— 0553804720

# 9. EXECUTIVE PRESENCE

1. UI/UX is an acronym for User interface / User experience. It is a key performance indicator for mobile phones, laptops, multimedia stations, websites, software, etc.

2. **Sylvia Ann Hewlett** is a Cambridge educated economist. An expert on gender and workplace issues, she works with

non-profit and governmental agencies to promote women in the workplace and lectures frequently around the world. To learn more https://book.11ceohabits.com/sylviaannhewlett

3. Executive Presence: The Missing Link Between Merit and Success. By Sylvia Ann Hewlett ISBN: 978-0062246899

4. **Robert Warren Dudley** is an American-born businessman who is a former group chief executive of British Petroleum. To learn more https://book.11ceohabits.com/bobdudley

5. Real Leaders Don't Do PowerPoint: How to Sell Yourself and Your Ideas. By Christopher Wittand Dale Fetherling. ISBN: 978-0307407702

6. Janine Schindler names Mahatma Gandhi as a figure with 'gravitas' in the blog article How To Develop 'Gravitas' And Boost Your Executive Presence. Gravitas is a component of executive presence. Janine Schindler is a Leadership Coach And Facilitator For The Left-Brained Analytical Leader & Founder of 'JAS Leadership'. https://book.11ceohabits.com/mahatmagandhi

7. Skip Prichard sketches the simplicity and authenticity of Nelson Mandela in the blog article 11 Leadership Qualities of Skip Prichard meets Nelson Mandela. https://book.11ceohabits.com/nelsonmandela Skip Prichard is an *Inc. Top 100 Leadership Speaker* and author of the **WSJ** bestselling book, *The Book of Mistakes: 9 Secrets to Creating a Successful Future.* He is known for his track record of successfully repositioning companies, dramatically improving results and corporate culture. He is a keynote speaker on topics ranging from leadership, personal development, growth strategies, culture, corporate turnarounds, and the future of publishing. His views have been featured in print and broadcast media including the BBC, The New York Times, CNN, NPR, The Daily Beast, Harvard Business Review, Fast Company, Writer's Digest, Information Today, Inc., The Bookseller, Publishers Weekly, Christian Retailing, Forbes, and the Library Journal.

8. Julie Hansen says, "Steve Jobs raised the bar on public speaking and executive presence for all of us". Reference blog article Executive Presence (When you Don't Wear Black Turtlenecks)http://book.11ceohabits.com/juliehansenarticle Julie Hansen is a Sales Presentation Expert and founder of Performance Sales and Training.

9. Ustadh Nouman Ali Khan is a Muslim speaker, Islamic scholar, and founder, CEO and lead instructor at Bayyinah,

the Institute for Arabic and Qur'anic Studies. A popular figure online with over 1.9 million Facebook followers, he is named one of the 500 most influential Muslims in the world by the Royal Islamic Strategic Studies Centre of Jordan. He lectures in English and Urdu https://book.11ceohabits.com/noumanalikhan

10. BK Shivani is a globally renowned YouTube celebrity, spiritual guide and mentor. She has 3 million subscribers and 318 million views of content. She lectures in English and Hindi. https://book.11ceohabits.com/bkshivani

11. Dr. Vandana Shiva is a physicist with a doctorate on the subject "Hidden Variables and Non-locality in Quantum Theory" from the University of Western Ontario in Canada. She later shifted to inter-disciplinary research in science, technology and environmental policy. Forbes magazine in November 2010 identified Vandana Shiva as one of the top Seven most Powerful Women on the Globe. Dr. Shiva has received honorary Doctorates from the University of Paris, University of Western Ontario, University of Oslo and Connecticut College, University of Guelph. Among her many awards are the Alternative Nobel Prize (Right Livelihood Award, 1993), Order of the Golden Ark, Global 500 Award of UN and Earth Day International Award, Lennon ONO grant for peace award by Yoko Ono, Sydney Peace Prize, Doshi Bridgebuilder Award, Calgary Peace Prize, Thomas Merton Award, the Fukuoka Award, The Prism of Reason Award, the Grifone d'Argento prize and The MIDORI Prize for Biodiversity. https://book.11ceohabits.com/vandanashiva The Navdanya movement was created by Dr. Vandana Shiva 30 years ago in India to defend seed and food sovereignty, and small farmers around the world. Navdanya pioneered the movement of seed saving and seed freedom, which began in response to the crisis of erosion of agricultural biodiversity and introduction of GMOs and patents on seeds through intellectual property rights (IPRs) and 'free trade' agreements. It is a voice against biopiracy and the patenting of indigenous knowledge by multinational corporations.

## 10. SPOTTING THE BLACK SWAN

1. **Nassim Nicholas Taleb** is an essayist, scholar, mathematical statistician, and former option trader and risk analyst, whose work concerns problems of randomness, probability, and uncertainty. His 2007 book *The Black Swan* has been described by *The Sunday Times* as one of the twelve most influential books since World War II. To learn more https://book.11ceohabits.com/nassimnicholastaleb

2. The Black Swan: The Impact of the Highly Improbable. By Nassim Nicholas Taleb ISBN: 978-0812973815

3. Chris Voss is an Ex-FBI Agent, Hostage Negotiator and Author of the book on negotiation 'Never Split The Difference'.

4. Stewardship is a term used in church sermons to describe the duty to administer God's resources with honesty, accountability, and responsibility.

5. KOL is an acronym for Key Opinion Leader. KOL is usually an individual with professional credibility and accomplishments. His opinions carry weight.

6. Never Split The Difference — Negotiating as if your life depended on it. By Chris Voss with Tahl Raz ISBN: 978— 0— 06— 240780— 1

7. Negotiation Genius — How to overcome obstacles and achieve brilliant results at the bargaining table and beyond. By Deepak Malhotra and Max H. Bazerman. eISBN: 978— 0— 55390494— 9

8. Getting (More Of) What You Want — How the secrets of economics and psychology can help you negotiate anything, in business and life. By Margaret A. Neale and Thomas Z. Lys ISBN: 978— 0— 465— 05072— 7 (hardcover) ISBN: 978— 0— 465— 04063— 6 (eBook)

9. Getting To Yes — Negotiating agreement without giving in. 2nd Edition. By Roger Fisher, William Try and Bruce Patton. ISBN: 978— 0— 14— 015735— 2

10. Getting Past No — Negotiating in difficult situations. By William Try. eISBN: 978— 0— 55390364— 5

## 11. ATTENTION TO DETAIL

1. Joseph Cardillo is a top-selling author in health, mind-body, and martial arts. His books Be Like Water and Bow to Life

have inspired people of all ages and backgrounds worldwide. As an educator, he has taught over 20,000 students at several colleges and universities, including the University at Albany and Hudson Valley Community College, where he is a professor of English and creative writing. He teaches classes in health and wellness at a wide range of other institutions, and has received two state university sabbaticals for work in consciousness studies. He regularly presents workshops and seminars based on his books. Joseph also writes a blog on attention training for Psychology Today. He and his family reside in New York state. https://book. 11ceohabits.com/josephcardillo

2. Miyamoto Musashi (宮本 武蔵, March 12, 1584, Ōhara-Chō, — June 13, 1645), also known as Shinmen Takezō, Miyamoto Bennosuke or, by his Buddhist name, Niten Dōraku, was a Japanese swordsman, philosopher, strategist, writer and rōnin. Musashi, as he was often simply known, became renowned through stories of his unique double-bladed swordsmanship and undefeated record in his 61 duels (next is 33 by Itō Ittōsai). He is considered a Kensei, a sword-saint of Japan.[3] He was the founder of the Niten Ichi-ryū school or Nito Ichi-ryū style of swordsmanship, and in his final years authored The Book of Five Rings (五輪の書, Go Rin No Sho), and Dokkōdō (The Path of Aloneness).

3. Reference text is from the book 'Can I Have Your Attention — How to think fast, find your focus and sharpen your concentration'. By Joseph Cardillo ISBN: 978— 1— 60163— 063— 6

4. Sensei, pronounced sen-say, is a Japanese word for a teacher. This includes instructors such as dance instructors and training instructors at a karate dojo, or martial arts school.

5. The term is shortened from **mushin no shin** (無心の心), a Zen expression meaning *the mind without mind* and is also referred to as the state of "no-mindness." That is, a mind not fixed or occupied by thought or emotion and thus open to everything. It is translated by D.T. Suzuki as "being free from mind-attachment." https://book.11ceohabits.com/mushin

6. Reference article Definition of Mushin https://book. 11ceohabits.com/mushindefinition

7. Hollywood movie The Last Samurai is a 2003 American period action drama film directed and co-produced by Edward Zwick. It grossed $456 million at the box office and was nom-

inated for several awards, including four Academy Awards, three Golden Globe Awards, and two National Board of Review Awards.

8. Chris Denny is a researcher, trainer, consultant, and author of Improve Attention To Detail: A straightforward system to develop attention to detail in yourself, employees, and across an organization which you can now buy on Amazon. The book is based on the research, surveys, interviews, and experience he brings to his live workshops and online courses https://book.11ceohabits.com/chrisdenny

9. Link to the video 'The 3 Types Of Attention To Detail' https://book.11ceohabits.com/attentionvideo

10. Link to video Change Blindness https://book.11ceohabits.com/changeblindness

11. Link to video Change Blindness https://book.11ceohabits.com/changeblindness

12. Max H Bazerman Co-director of the Center for Public Leadership at the Harvard Kennedy School, the Straus Professor at the Harvard Business School, and the author of numerous books, including Negotiation Genius with Deepak Malhotra, Blind Spots with Ann E. Tenbrunsel, and Judgment in Managerial Decision Making with Don A. Moore. He has taught, advised companies, and consulted to governments in thirty countries. He is on numerous editorial boards. He has received an honorary doctorate from the University of London, the Life Achievement Award from the Aspen Institute's Business and Society Program, and the Distinguished Educator Award from the Academy of Management, among many other awards.

13. The Power Of Noticing — What the best leaders see. By Max H. Bazerman. ISBN: 978— 1— 4767— 0029— 8 (print book) ISBN: 978— 1— 47670031— 1 (eBook)

14. Mahzarin Rustum Banaji FBA is an American psychologist at Harvard University, known for her work popularizing the concept of implicit bias in regards to race, gender, sexual orientation, and other factors. https://book.11ceohabits.com/mahzarinbanaji

15. Ulric Gustav Neisser was a German-born American psychologist and member of the US National Academy of Sciences. He has been referred to as the "father of cognitive psychology". Neisser researched and wrote about perception and memory. https://book.11ceohabits.com/ulricneisser

16. Link to the video The Monkey Business Illusion https://book.11ceohabits.com/monkeybusiness

17. Frenemy is a friend who sometimes behaves like an enemy.

18. Joseph Cardillo is a top-selling author in health, mind-body, and martial arts. His books Be Like Water and Bow to Life have inspired people of all ages and backgrounds worldwide. As an educator, he has taught over 20,000 students at several colleges and universities, including the University at Albany and Hudson Valley Community College, where he is a professor of English and creative writing. He teaches classes in health and wellness at a wide range of other institutions, and has received two state university sabbaticals for work in consciousness studies. He regularly presents workshops and seminars based on his books. Joseph also writes a blog on attention training for Psychology Today. He and his family reside in New York state. https://book.11ceohabits.com/josephcardillo

19. Marco Arment (born June 11, 1982) is an American iOS developer and web developer, podcaster, technology writer and former magazine editor. https://book.11ceohabits.com/marcoarment, https://book.11ceohabits.com/marcoarmentwebsite

# 12. RELATIONSHIPS FOR LIFE

1. ROI is an acronym for Return on Investment. It measures the cumulative value delivered by the product.

2. Meaning of ethos — The characteristic spirit of a culture, era, or community as manifested in its beliefs and aspirations. https://book.11ceohabits.com/ethos

3. Sheikh Mohammed bin Rashid Al Maktoum is the Vice President and Prime Minister of the United Arab Emirates (UAE), and ruler of the Emirate of Dubai. He is simply called Sheikh Mohammed in local media coverage. To learn more https://book.11ceohabits.com/sheikhmohammed

4. The United Nations places UAE among top three countries with the highest percent of immigrants. https://book.11ceohabits.com/UNranking

5. 80% of UAE's residents are immigrants from over 200 countries, only 20% are native citizens. https://book.11ceohabits.com/expatriatesuae

6. The Sheikh CEO — Lessons in leadership from Mohammed Bin Rashid Al Maktoum. By Dr. Yasar Jarrar ISBN: 978— 1 — 78596— 110— 6

7. Watch: Sheikh Mohammed finds empty office during government spot-checks. By Arabian Business https://book.11ceohabits.com/emptyoffice

8. Sheikh Mohammed Sacks Government Officials After Finding Their Desks Empty. By Jack Rogers, Emirates Woman https://book.11ceohabits.com/emptydesks

9. Wooden Spoon is an award given to an individual or team who/which has come last in a competition. The wooden spoon was presented originally at the University of Cambridge by the students to the man who achieved the lowest exam marks but still earned a *junior optime* in the Mathematical Tripos. In United States' men's Major League Soccer, the last place team in the overall standings is considered as the "wooden spoon champion". A wooden spoon, also known as the "anti-slam", is sometimes spoken about in tennis. It is described as the worst possible outcome in a tournament, applying to the player for whom the following scenario occurs:

   Won by the player who is defeated in the first round by a player who is defeated in the second round, who is defeated in the third round and so forth, until the final of a given tournament. In the Cambridge and Oxford Bumps races, a crew who get bumped each day (thus moving down four places) are awarded spoons. The term is commonly used in Australian and New Zealand sporting competitions, most notably in the major Australian rules, soccer, rugby league and rugby union leagues (such as the AFL, the A-League, NRL, Super Rugby and ITM Cup) and refers to the club positioned last on the league table at the end of the season. https://book.11ceohabits.com/woodenspoon

10. Sheikh Mohammed lists UAE's worst, best service centres. Khaleej Times https://book.11ceohabits.com/uaebestworst

11. UAE's five best and worst government centers revealed. Bahrain News Agency https://book.11ceohabits.com/uaebestworstreport

12. Sheikh Hamdan gives worst government departments two weeks for turnaround plan. By Patrick Ryan, The National https://book.11ceohabits.com/twoweeks

13. Dubai Cares supports education initiatives for under-privileged communities and individuals across the globe. To learn more https://book.11ceohabits.com/dubaicares

14. Mentioned by the author in The Sheikh CEO — Lessons in leadership from Mohammed Bin Rashid Al Maktoum. By Dr. Yasar Jarrar ISBN: 978— 1— 78596— 110— 6

15. Reference article Farewell party for those who can't join the development march, says UAE Vice-President. By Zaher Bitar, Gulf News https://book.11ceohabits.com/farewellparty

16. Reference news article **UAE named one of the safest countries in the world**. By Colin Armstrong. https://book.11ceohabits.com/safest

17. The 2020 Global Law and Order Report was based on 175,000+ interviews with residents in 144+ countries. Reference web page WORLD POLL - Gallup's Global Law and Order Research Center https://book.11ceohabits.com/galluplawandorder

18. Reference news article **Dubai and Abu Dhabi named among the best cities in the world.** By Colin Armstrong. https://book.11ceohabits.com/bestcities

19. **Bloomberg** delivers business and markets news, data, analysis, and video to the world, featuring stories from Businessweek and Bloomberg News.

20. Reference Web page - 2021 WORLD'S BEST CITIES https://book.11ceohabits.com/bestcities2021

21. Yasar Jarrar, PhD, has worked at The Executive Office of Sheikh Mohammed Bin Rashid Al Maktoum in various roles spanning UAE and Dubai governments. He is an expert in strategy, public policy and innovation.

22. The Sheikh CEO — Lessons in leadership from Mohammed Bin Rashid Al Maktoum. By Dr. Yasar Jarrar ISBN: 978— 1 — 78596— 110— 6

23. The Edelman Trust Barometer is an annual credibility and trust survey conducted by Edelman Intelligence, a global insight and analytics consultancy. https://book.11ceohabits.com/edelmantrustbarometer

24. Witold Pilecki was a cavalry officer, intelligence agent, and resistance leader. During World War II, he volunteered to be captured by the Nazis and embedded in Auschwitz concentration camp, to understand the nature of the camp, which was not known at the time. After his escape several years later, he wrote *Witold's Report*, the first comprehensive intelligence report on the atrocities of the Holocaust.

25. Auschwitz was a Nazi concentration camp operated during World War II and the Holocaust. Of the 1.3 million people

sent to Auschwitz, 1.1 million died. Those not gassed died of starvation, exhaustion, disease, individual executions, or beatings. Others were killed during medical experiments. https://en.wikipedia.org/wiki/Auschwitz_concentration_camp#Tattoos_and_triangles

26. Everything Is F*cked: A Book about Hope. By Mark Manson. ISBN: 978— 0062888433


# 13. THE 12TH NON-HABIT

1. A message to Garcia is an endearing essay in charming prose, written by Elbert Hubbard in 1899. It captured the hearts of millions across several nations. To learn more https://book.11ceohabits.com/garcia

2. **Elbert Green Hubbard** (June 19, 1856 — May 7, 1915) was an American writer, publisher, artist, and philosopher. To learn more https://book.11ceohabits.com/elberthubbard

3. 1st Lt. Andrew S. Rowan was an American army officer who served in the Spanish-American War, the Philippine War, and the Moro Rebellion, and became famous for reportedly delivering a message to Gen. Calixto Garcia in Cuba. To learn more https://book.11ceohabits.com/rowan

4. President William McKinley was the 25th President of the United States from 1897 until his assassination in 1901. To learn more https://book.11ceohabits.com/williammckinley

5. **Calixto García Íñiguez** (August 4, 1839 — December 11, 1898) was a Cuban general in three Cuban uprisings, part of the Cuban War for Independence: the Ten Years' War, the Little War, and the War of 1895, itself sometimes called the Cuban War for Independence, which bled into the Spanish-American War, ultimately resulting in national independence for Cuba. To learn more https://book.11ceohabits.com/calixto

6. Spanish-American War - to learn more https://book.11ceohabits.com/war

7. Download link to The Project Gutenberg eBook of A Message to Garcia, by Elbert Hubbard https://book.11ceohabits.com/bookfunnelgarcia

# 14. THE SECRET KPIS

1. Anne Sullivan was the teacher and lifelong companion to Helen Keller. She contracted an eye disease at age five and was visually impaired. She spent a large part of her childhood in dismal living conditions. However, it did not dampen her fiery spirit. A series of eye operations significantly improved her vision. She graduated from the Perkins School for the Blind at age 20 and became a teacher to Helen Keller. She was able to cope with the curiosity, tantrums and defiance of Helen Keller. She taught alphabets, words and sentences by connecting to Helen Keller's inner world. To learn more https://book.11ceohabits.com/annesullivan

2. Helen Keller was born deaf and blind. This means she could not speak and she could not hear and she could not see. She overcame these limitations to be an author, political activist, and lecturer. To learn more https://book.11ceohabits.com/helenkeller

3. Link to The Miracle Worker — Helen's First Lesson https://book.11ceohabits.com/miracleworker

4. **Sir Roger Gilbert Bannister** (23 March 1929 — 3 March 2018) was a British middle-distance athlete and neurologist who ran the first sub-4-minute mile. To learn more https://book.11ceohabits.com/rogerbannister

5. Reference blog article What Breaking the 4-Minute Mile Taught Us About the Limits of Conventional Thinking. By Bill Taylor, Harvard Business Review https://book.11ceohabits.com/4minutemile

6. Reference book 3:59.4: The Quest to Break the 4 Minute Mile. By John Bryant ISBN: 978— 0099469087

7. Meaning of consternation — Feelings of anxiety or dismay, typically at something unexpected. To learn more https://book.11ceohabits.com/consternation

8. Stanford study: Evaluating Information: The Cornerstone Of Civic Online Reasoning https://book.11ceohabits.com/stanfordstudy

9. Stanford web page for the study on civic online reasoning https://purl.stanford.edu/fv751yt5934

10. Butterfly effect is a phenomenon wherein a small change in conditions can lead to vastly different outcomes. Understanding the butterfly effect provides the perspective to view

business, markets, and more. To learn more https://book.11ceohabits.com/butterflyeffect

11. A study by MindEdge — a learning company founded by Harvard and MIT educators — shares that 64% of millennials thought critical thinking skills are important for their future job prospects. Yet, only 36% of millennials felt they are well trained in this area, even though most studied the subject in college. To learn more https://book.11ceohabits.com/mindedgestudy

12. MindEdge is a learning company founded by Harvard and MIT educators. To learn more https://book.11ceohabits.com/mindedge

13. Hemingway Editor makes your writing concise and clear. To learn more https://book.11ceohabits.com/hemingway

14. ProWritingAid — A grammar checker, style editor, and writing mentor in one package. To learn more https://prowritingaid.com

15. Grammarly Get corrections from Grammarly while you write on Gmail, Twitter, LinkedIn, and all other favorite sites. To learn more https://book.11ceohabits.com/grammarly

16. A no— no is anything that is forbidden or not advisable. To learn more https://book.11ceohabits.com/no

17. Harakiri was practised in Japan by samurai as an honourable alternative to disgrace or execution. It involves ritual suicide by disembowelment with a sword. Creative harakiri implies killing the creative impact of content through errors.

18. Maria Konnikova is a Russian— American writer and psychologist. She has a B.A. in psychology and creative writing from Harvard University and a Ph.D. in psychology from Columbia University. She has worked as a television producer, written for several magazines and online publications, and authored two *New York Times* best— selling books. She primarily writes about psychology and its application to real life situations. Maria Konnikova is the author of 'The Confidence Game' and 'Mastermind: How to Think Like Sherlock Holmes'. To learn more https://en.wikipedia.org/wiki/Maria_Konnikova

19. Blog article How People Learn to Become Resilient by Maria Konnikova. To learn more https://book.11ceohabits.com/mariakonnikovablog

20. SOP is an acronym for Standard Operating Procedure. SOP means the documentation of company processes and proce-

dures. It helps establish clarity on steps to follow, who's in charge, etc.

SOPs are helpful for **Onboarding Employees** – Documentation makes it easy for new hires to get up to speed on processes, protocol and procedures. **Enforcing Best Practices** – SOPs clarify which processes are the "best practice" and reveal the ones who flout these frequently.

These benefits impact business and make task handling efficient. To learn more https://book.11ceohabits.com/sop

21. Finablr on Wikipedia https://book.11ceohabits.com/wikifinablr

22. Former Travelex owner Finablr finds new owner after tough year. Evening Express. To learn more https://book.11ceohabits.com/finablr

# 15. THE CEO'S INNER CIRCLE

1. Responses to the question 'Which do you prefer: wisdom or intelligence?' On Quora https://book.11ceohabits.com/wisdomorintelligence

2. **Wisdom** (Wikipedia first paragraph as at 22/06/18):
   Wisdom or sapience is the ability to think and act using knowledge, experience, understanding, common sense, and insight, especially in a mature or utilitarian manner. There appears to be consensus that wisdom is associated with attributes such as compassion, experiential self-knowledge, non-attachment and virtues such as ethics and benevolence. To learn more https://book.11ceohabits.com/wisdom

3. **Intelligence** (Wikipedia first paragraph as at 22/06/18):
   Intelligence has been defined in different ways to include the capacity for logic, understanding, self-awareness, learning, emotional knowledge, reasoning, planning, creativity, and problem solving. It can be more generally described as the ability to perceive or infer information, and to retain it as knowledge to be applied towards adaptive behaviors within an environment or context. To learn more https://book.11ceohabits.com/intelligence

4. Anne Cregan's page on Quora https://book.11ceohabits.com/annecregan

5. Ivan William Kelly is a Professor at University of Saskatchewan, Saskatoon, Canada. He has university background in psychology, mathematics/statistics, research

methods and philosophy (extensive philosophy coursework at both undergraduate and graduate levels). Other interests are world history, cognitive psychology, ethics, non-Western philosophy, technology and society, philosophy of science, science fiction and world literature. He is an interdisciplinary scholar with articles in leading journals in several different fields including mathematics, philosophy and psychology. To learn more https://book.11ceohabits.com/ivankelly

6. A virtue is a trait or quality that is valued as a foundation of principle and good moral being. Personal virtues are characteristics that promote collective and individual greatness. To learn more https://book.11ceohabits.com/virtue

7. Kelly, Ivan. (2018). Re: Is intelligence or wisdom more useful?. Retrieved from: https://book.11ceohabits.com/intelligentcriminals.

8. Trump card — the Joker in a deck of playing cards is the trump card. It is capable of changing the outcomes of the game. To learn more https://book.11ceohabits.com/trump

9. The knight of a chess game — Compared to other chess pieces, the knight's movement is unique. While moving, the knight can jump over pieces to reach its destination. To learn more https://en.wikipedia.org/wiki/Knight_(chess)

10. If you hide your light under a bushel, you keep your abilities or good qualities hidden from other people. To learn more https://book.11ceohabits.com/bushel

11. Sentinel event — an unanticipated event in a healthcare setting resulting in death or serious injury to a patient, not related to the natural course of the patient's illness.

12. Real Time is something that is occurring immediately. To learn more https://book.11ceohabits.com/realtime

13. See Chapter 13, section Carry a message to Garcia.

14. Dance to your own drummer means you are your own standard. To learn more https://book.11ceohabits.com/drummer

15. Yoona Kang is the Research Director of the Communication Neuroscience Lab in the Annenberg School for Communication at the University of Pennsylvania. Her research investigates psychological and neural mechanisms that support the development and changes in social cognition, emotions, and health outcomes. Kang received her B.A. in Psychology from UCLA and Ph.D. in Psychology from Yale University. To learn more https://book.11ceohabits.com/yoonakang

16. Quoted from the article Thinking beyond yourself can make you more open to healthy lifestyle choices https://book. 11ceohabits.com/thinkbeyondself
17. Viktor Emil Frankl was a neurologist, psychiatrist, Holocaust survivor and founder of logotherapy (literally "healing through meaning"). To learn more https://en.wikipedia.org/wiki/Viktor_Frankl
18. Quote source https://doctorjosegomez.com/think— beyond — add— meaning— happier— life/
19. Viktor Emil Frankl was a neurologist, psychiatrist, Holocaust survivor and founder of logotherapy (literally "healing through meaning"). To learn more https://en.wikipedia.org/wiki/Viktor_Frankl
20. The book Man's Search for Meaning chronicles the experiences of Viktor Frankl as a prisoner in Nazi concentration camps during World War II, and describe his psychotherapeutic method, which involved identifying a purpose in life to feel positive about, and then immersively imagining that outcome. To learn more https://en.wikipedia.org/wiki/Man%27s_Search_for_Meaning

## 17. THE GRAYSCALE EMPLOYEE

1. Author Katherine Ramsland teaches forensic psychology at DeSales University in Pennsylvania. She is a feature writer for Court TV's Crime Library and has written more than 300 articles about serial killers, forensic psychology and forensic science. https://book.11ceohabits.com/katherineramsland
2. Inside The Minds Of Healthcare Serial Killers — Why they kill. By Katherine Ramsland ISBN: 978— 0— 275— 99422— 8
3. John Camp is a New York Times best— selling author, American novelist, a former journalist and recipient of the Pulitzer Prize. https://book.11ceohabits.com/johncamp
4. One Hundred Years Of Medical Murder. By John Camp ISBN: 978— 0586056172
5. Author Katherine Ramsland teaches forensic psychology at DeSales University in Pennsylvania. She is a feature writer for Court TV's Crime Library and has written more than 300 articles about serial killers, forensic psychology and forensic science. https://book.11ceohabits.com/katherineramsland

6. Inside The Minds Of Healthcare Serial Killers — Why they kill. By Katherine Ramsland ISBN: 978— 0— 275— 99422— 8

7. One Hundred Years Of Medical Murder. By John Camp ISBN: 978— 0586056172

8. Columbia Hospital Corporation / Hospital Corporation Of America is an American for-profit operator of health care facilities that owns and operates 186 hospitals and approximately 2,000 sites of care, including surgery centers, freestanding emergency rooms, urgent care centers and physician clinics in 21 US states and the United Kingdom. In 1993, lawsuits were filed against HCA by former employees who alleged that the company had engaged in questionable Medicare billing practices. In 1997, a federal investigation was initiated by the FBI, the IRS and the Department of Health and Human Services. The federal probe culminated in 2003 with "the government receiving a total of over $2 billion in criminal fines and civil penalties for systematically defrauding federal health care programs." Columbia/HCA pleaded guilty to 14 felonies and admitted to systematically overcharging the government. The federal probe has been referred to as the longest and costliest investigation for health care fraud in US history. To learn more https://book.11ceohabits.com/hcascam

9. Undercover — How I went from company man to FBI spy and exposed the worst healthcare fraud in US history. By John W. Schilling. ISBN: 978— 1452055084

10. Graden-variety means of the usual or ordinary type; commonplace.

11. Inventory that doesn't turn over – that doesn't sell – is often referred to as dead stock. With businesses that don't use inventory management software, dead stock can remain on warehouse shelves forgotten and useless. To learn more https://book.11ceohabits.com/deadstock

12. The **deadwood employee** is the one who routinely does the minimum amount to get by, often blaming others or the "system" when there are problems. They may have "retired on the job," while waiting for the official end to their work career, or simply lost motivation long ago. To learn more https://book.11ceohabits.com/deadwood

13. Reference blog article 'Dealing with energy-sucking 'deadwood' employees https://book.11ceohabits.com/deadwood

14. Sinister means someone who is a threatening or portending evil, harm, or trouble.
15. Fiefdom is a territory or sphere of operation controlled by a particular person or group.
16. To rub someone the wrong way means annoy, anger or irritate them.
17. Lifescripts: What to say to get what you want in life's toughest situations. Stephen M. Pollan and Mark Levine. ISBN — 978 — 1119571971, 0— 471— 63101— 9 (trade edition), 0— 471— 64376— 9 (special edition with CD).
18. Paul Babiak and Robert D. Hare are the authors of Snakes in Suits — When psychopaths go to work.

# 18. PERSONAL POWER

1. A low-ball offer is a slang term for an offer that is significantly below the seller's asking price, or a quote that is deliberately lower than the price the seller intends to charge. https://book.11ceohabits.com/lowball
2. Munchausen's syndrome is a psychological disorder where someone pretends to be ill or deliberately produces symptoms of illness in themselves. Their main intention is to assume the "sick role" so that people care for them and they are the centre of attention. To learn more https://book.11ceohabits.com/munchausen
3. **Munchausen syndrome by proxy** (MSBP) is a mental health problem in which a caregiver makes up or causes an illness or injury in a person under his or her care, such as a child, an elderly adult, or a person who has a disability. Because vulnerable people are the victims, MSBP is a form of child abuse or elder abuse. To learn more https://book.11ceohabits.com/munchausenproxy
4. A flat line refers to either a flatlined electrocardiogram, where the heart shows no electrical activity or to a flat electroencephalogram, in which the brain shows no electrical activity. These cases are involved in various definitions of death. To learn more https://book.11ceohabits.com/flatline
5. Dissociation with the self is termed as Dissociative Identity Disorder in clinical psychology and psychiatry. To learn more https://book.11ceohabits.com/disorder
6. Great Place To Work Certification™ recognizes companies who have built high-trust, high-performance company cul-

tures. To learn more https://book.11ceohabits.com/greatplacetowork

7. To be in limbo means being caught between two stages and it is unclear what will happen next.

8. To be on tenterhooks means waiting nervously for something to happen.

9. Shahida Arabi is a graduate of Columbia University graduate school. She is the bestselling author of The Smart Girl's Guide to Self-Care and author of Becoming the Narcissist's Nightmare: How to Devalue and Discard the Narcissist While Supplying Yourself, featured as a #1 Amazon Bestseller in three categories. She studied Psychology and English Literature as an undergraduate at NYU, where she graduated summa cum laude. Her interests include psychology, sociology, education, gender studies and mental health advocacy. Huff Post https://book.11ceohabits.com/shahidaarabi

10. Link to blog article 20 Diversion Tactics Highly Manipulative Narcissists, Sociopaths And Psychopaths Use To Silence You https://book.11ceohabits.com/tactics

11. Confessions of a Sociopath: A Life Spent Hiding in Plain Sight. By M.E. Thomas. ISBN: 978-0307956651

12. Reference blog **49 Secrets Your Boss Won't Tell You— But You Need to Know** https://book.11ceohabits.com/secrets

13. Lifescripts - refer Chapter 3, subheading Lifescripts

14. Comebacks - refer Chapter 3, subheading The Great Comeback

15. Black Swans - refer Chapter 10 Spotting the black swan

16. Marie G. McIntyre, PH.D. has over twenty years' experience in management, leadership development, and career coaching. She is the author of Secrets to Winning at Office Politics and The Management Team Handbook. To learn more https://book.11ceohabits.com/mariemcintyre

17. Secrets to Winning at Office Politics: How to Achieve Your Goals and Increase Your Influence at Work. By Marie G. McIntyre ISBN: 978-0312332181

18. Becoming the Narcissist's Nightmare: How to Devalue and Discard the Narcissist While Supplying yourself. By Shahida Arabi. ISBN: 978-1523702466

## 19. THE BURNING QUESTION

1. The study of organizational behavior gives insight on how employees behave and perform at the workplace.
2. Krista Wolfe is a search engine optimization (SEO) professional. Reference blog The Most Stolen Supplies: And how to prevent Office Supply Theft https://book.11ceohabits.com/stolensupplies
3. Rene Chun is a contributing editor at Wired. Reference blog Criminal Tendencies — Workplace Theft Is On The Rise https://book.11ceohabits.com/renechun
4. Yannieck Griep is the Assistant Professor of Industrial and Organizational Psychology at the University of Calgary. Reference blog 'This is why everyone steals office supplies from work — including you' https://book.11ceohabits.com/stealsupplies
5. A psychological contract is the employee's viewpoint of reciprocal obligation between the individual and the organization. To learn more, view Psychological and Implied Contracts In Organisations https://book.11ceohabits.com/psychologicalcontract
6. Cognitive dissonance is the mental discomfort experienced by an individual when new information contradicts a belief held by the individual.
7. Witold Pilecki was a cavalry officer, intelligence agent, and resistance leader. During World War II, he volunteered to be captured by the Nazis and embedded in Auschwitz concentration camp, to understand the nature of the camp, which was not known at the time. After his escape several years later, he wrote *Witold's Report,* the first comprehensive intelligence report on the atrocities of the Holocaust. To learn more https://book.11ceohabits.com/witoldpilecki
8. Auschwitz was a Nazi concentration camp operated during World War II and the Holocaust. Of the 1.3 million people sent to Auschwitz, 1.1 million died. Those not gassed died of starvation, exhaustion, disease, individual executions, or beatings. Others were killed during medical experiments. To learn more https://book.11ceohabits.com/auschwitz
9. Back story on Captain Witold Pilecki is in Chapter 12 - Relationships for Life, Sub heading - An Extreme Example.

10. Frank Abagnale is an American security consultant known for his career as a con man, check forger and impostor. To learn more https://book.11ceohabits.com/frankabagnale

11. Reference article Fraud Watch Ambassador Named https://book.11ceohabits.com/ambassador

12. Link The Perfect Scam podcast page https://book.11ceohabits.com/perfectscampodcast

13. Nepotism is the practice among those with power or influence of favoring *relatives* by giving them jobs.

14. Cronyism is the practice among those with power or influence of favoring *friends* by giving them jobs.

15. Khatri N., Tsang E.W.K. (2016) Antecedents and Consequences of Cronyism in Organizations. In: Khatri N., Ojha A.K. (eds) Crony Capitalism in India. Palgrave Studies in Indian Management. Palgrave Macmillan, London. https://book.11ceohabits.com/cronycapitalism

16. The Asian financial crisis of 1997 started in Thailand. Indonesia, South Korea and Thailand were the countries most affected by the crisis. Hong Kong, Laos, Malaysia and Philippines were also hurt by the slump. To learn more https://book.11ceohabits.com/asianfinancialcrisis

17. Tim Pile has written over 300 travel articles for the South China Morning Post. He has been to over 100 countries and has a Master's degree in Tourism Environment and Development. Reference blog article 'Who are the World's Worst Tourists?' https://book.11ceohabits.com/worsttourists

18. Dana Wilkie is the Online Manager and Editor for Employee Relations content at the Society for Human Resources Management (SHRM). Reference blog article When HR Gets It Wrong: Misconduct Won't Change Until The Culture Does https://book.11ceohabits.com/misconduct

19. Bridget Miller is a contributing editor of the HR Management & Compliance category in the blog HR Daily Advisor. To learn more https://book.11ceohabits.com/bridgetmiller

20. **J. Harold Ellens** (16 July 1932 — 13 April 2018) was a psychologist and theologian. He was the founding editor of the *Journal of Psychology and Christianity* and also the Executive Director of the Christian Association for Psychological Studies International from 1974 to 1989. He was one of the key figures in psychological biblical criticism and served as Chair of the Psychology and Biblical Studies Section of the Society of Biblical Literature. To learn more https://book.11ceohabits.com/haroldellens

21.  Explaining Evil. By J. Harold Ellens. ISBN: 978-0313387159

# 20. HEART SPEAK

1.  Stanford study: Evaluating Information: The Cornerstone Of Civic Online Reasoning https://book.11ceohabits.com/stanfordstudy

2.  A stuffed shirt is someone who behaves in a very formal and old-fashioned way and thinks that they are very important. https://book.11ceohabits.com/stuffedshirt

3.  **Nafs** (نَفْس) is an Arabic word literally meaning 'self', and has been translated as "psyche", "ego". The term is cognate with the Hebrew word *nephesh*, נֶפֶשׁ To learn more https://book.11ceohabits.com/nafs

4.  Rumi was a 13th-century Persian poet, faqih, Islamic scholar, theologian, and Sufi mystic originally from Greater Khorasan in Greater Iran. Rumi's influence transcends national borders and ethnic divisions: Iranians, Tajiks, Turks, Greeks, Pashtuns, other Central Asian Muslims, and the Muslims of the Indian subcontinent have greatly appreciated his spiritual legacy for the past seven centuries. To learn more https://book.11ceohabits.com/rumi

5.  Rosary refers to the string of knots or beads used to count prayers and religious recitations. To learn more https://book.11ceohabits.com/rosary

6.  Al-Insān al-Kāmil means 'the person who has reached perfection', literally "the complete person". To learn more https://book.11ceohabits.com/alinsanalkamil

7.  Narottam is a word in Sanskrit language. It signifies the highest qualities of man, the one who is foremost among men.

8.  Qalb is the spiritual heart. Reference article Spiritual Heart: its dimensions, states, maltreatment, and remedies. To learn more https://book.11ceohabits.com/qalb

9.  Source: Wikipedia — Oskar Schindler was an industrialist who wanted to benefit from the Nazi regime. He transformed from capitalist to savior of thousands of Jews at great risk to his life. He spent his money to bribe officials and keep Jews safe from being taken to concentration camps. To learn more https://book.11ceohabits.com/oskarschindler

10. Source: Quora — Who was a notable person that was originally evil, but eventually regretted their evil and became good later on? https://book.11ceohabits.com/evilbecamegood
11. Source: Wikipedia — Schindler's List https://book.11ceohabits.com/schindlerslist
12. Source: Quora — Who was a notable person that was originally evil, but eventually regretted their evil and became good later on? https://book.11ceohabits.com/evilbecamegood
13. Moses the Black (330-405), also known as Abba Moses the Robber, the Ethiopian , and the Strong, was an ascetic monk and priest in Egypt. He converted from a life of crime to one of asceticism. To learn more https://book.11ceohabits.com/mosestheblack
14. General Butt Naked was a murderer and cannibal who received deliverance and gave up the acts of evil. To learn more https://book.11ceohabits.com/buttnaked
15. Source: Quora — Who was a notable person that was originally evil, but eventually regretted their evil and became good later on? https://book.11ceohabits.com/evilbecamegood
16. Source: Wikipedia — Nathan Bedford Forrest was a racist and head of Ku Klux Klan who amended his ways. To learn more https://book.11ceohabits.com/nathanforrest
17. Source: Quora — Who was a notable person that was originally evil, but eventually regretted their evil and became good later on? https://book.11ceohabits.com/evilbecamegood
18. Angulimala was a murderer who attained the highest level of sainthood in Buddhist faith. To learn more https://book.11ceohabits.com/angulimala
19. Source: Quora — Who was a notable person that was originally evil, but eventually regretted their evil and became good later on? https://book.11ceohabits.com/evilbecamegood
20. Frank Abagnale is an American security consultant known for his career as a con man, check forger and impostor. To learn more https://book.11ceohabits.com/frankabagnale
21. Quote source https://book.11ceohabits.com/viktorfranklquote


## 22. WHY I WROTE THIS BOOK


1. Reference video Hillary Yip on Entrepreneurship https://book.11ceohabits.com/yiptips

2. **Suhas Gopinath** is the founder, CEO, and Chairman of Globals Inc., a multinational IT company. He took charge as CEO at the age of 17, three years after founding the company. At the time, he was the world's youngest CEO. To learn more https://book.11ceohabits.com/suhasgopinath

# CREDITS

1. Shabnam Mohammad Ateeq Ansari is the Chief Knowledge Officer at a global distribution network serving education, life sciences, and medical technology verticals. She is a Certified Professional in Talent Development (CPTD®) from the Association for Talent Development (ATD). She is a Project Management Professional (PMP®) certified by the Project Management Institute (PMI). She has a postgraduate degree in Business Administration with specializations in Marketing & Human Resources. She is a Professional Reader & Reviewer for books in the genres — business, self-help and workplace culture. https://book.11ceohabits.com/ansarishabnamateeq
2. Pixabay https://book.11ceohabits.com/pixabay
3. Public Domain Vectors https://book.11ceohabits.com/publicdomainvectors
4. Freepik https://book.11ceohabits.com/freepik
5. Seekpng https://book.11ceohabits.com/seekpng
6. FlyClipArt https://book.11ceohabits.com/flyclipart
7. Pngwing https://book.11ceohabits.com/pngwing
8. Favpng https://book.11ceohabits.com/favpng
9. Clipartmax https://book.11ceohabits.com/clipartmax
10. Clipart-Library https://book.11ceohabits.com/clipartlibrary
11. PNGkey https://book.11ceohabits.com/pngkey
12. DLpng https://book.11ceohabits.com/dlpng
13. ClipartKey https://book.11ceohabits.com/clipartkey
14. WebstockReview https://book.11ceohabits.com/webstockreview
15. PNGio https://book.11ceohabits.com/pngio
16. WPclipart https://book.11ceohabits.com/wpclipart
17. NicePNG https://book.11ceohabits.com/nicepng
18. Vecteezy https://book.11ceohabits.com/vecteezy
19. https://book.11ceohabits.com/tracer
20. https://book.11ceohabits.com/imagecompress
21. https://book.11ceohabits.com/fontsquirrel

22. https://book.11ceohabits.com/fontspace
23. https://book.11ceohabits.com/Inkscape
24. https://book.11ceohabits.com/vellum
25. ProWritingAid — A grammar checker, style editor, and writing mentor in one package. https://book.11ceohabits.com/prowritingaid
26. https://book.11ceohabits.com/mockup— shots

# THE READING LIST

1. **Lifescripts: What to say to get what you want in life's toughest situations.** *Stephen M. Pollan and Mark Levine. ISBN — 978— 1119571971, 978—0— 471— 63101— 9*

2. **Workscripts: Perfect Phrases for High-Stakes Conversations.** *Stephen M. Pollan and Mark Levine. ISBN — 978— 0— 470— 63324— 3*

3. **Exactly What To Say — The Magic Words For Influence And Impact.** *By Phil M Jones. ISBN: 978— 0— 692— 88195— 8 (paperback) ISBN: 978— 0— 692— 88196— 5 (eBook)*

4. **How To Win Any Argument — Without Raising Your Voice, Losing Your Cool, Or Coming To Blows.** *By Robert Mayer ISBN: 978— 1601631817*

5. **Sensation & Perception.** *10th Edition. By E. Bruce Goldstein, James Brockmole. ISBN: 978— 1305580299*

6. **Sleights of Mind.** *By Stephen L. Macknik and Susana Martinez-Conde ISBN: 978-0312611675*

7. **Spy Secrets That Can Save Your Life: A Former CIA Officer Reveals Safety and Survival Techniques to Keep You and Your Family Protected.** *By Jason Hanson. ISBN: 978-0399175671*

8. **What Every BODY Is Saying — An ex-FBI agent's guide to speed reading people.** *By Joe Navarro with Marvin Karlins. ISBN: 978— 0— 06— 164486— 3*

9. **The Body Language Advantage — Maximize your personal and professional relationships with this ultimate photo guide to deciphering what others are secretly saying, in any situation.** *By Lillian Glass. ISBN: 978— 1— 59233— 515— 2 eISBN: 978— 1— 61058— 407— 4*

10. **Body Language — Learn how to read others and communicate with confidence.** *By Elizabeth Kuhnke. ISBN: 9780857087041 (print), 9780857087034*

11. **The Silent Language Of Leaders — How body language can help or hurt how you lead.** *By Carol Kinsey Goman. ISBN: 978— 0— 470— 87636— 7*

12. **Reading People — How to understand people and predict their behavior, anytime, anyplace.** *By Jo-Ellan Dimitrius and Mark Mazzarella. ISBN: 978— 0— 345— 50413— 5*

13. **The Definitive Book of Body Language — The hidden meaning behind people's gestures and expressions.** *By Allan & Barbara Pease. ISBN: 978— 0553804720*

14. **I Can Read You Like A Book — How to spot the messages and emotions people are really sending with their body language.** *By Gregory Hartley and Maryann Karinch. ISBN: 978— 156414— 941— 1*

15. **You Say More Than You Think — A 7-day plan for using the new body language to get what you want.** *By Janine Driver with Mariska van Aalst. eISBN: 978— 0— 307— 45399— 0*

16. **Winning Body Language — Control the conversation, command attention and convey the right message — without saying a word.** *By Mark Bowden. ISBN: 978— 0— 07— 170164— 8*

17. **Without Saying A Word — Master the science of body language & maximize your success.** *By Kasia Wezowski and Patrick Wezowski. ISBN: 978— 0— 8144— 3974— 6 (eBook)*

18. **Executive Presence: The Missing Link Between Merit and Success.** *By Sylvia Ann Hewlett ISBN: 978-0062246899*

19. **Real Leaders Don't Do PowerPoint: How to Sell Yourself and Your Ideas.** *By Christopher Witt and Dale Fetherling. ISBN: 978-0307407702*

20. **Never Split The Difference — Negotiating as if your life depended on it.** *By Chris Voss with Tahl Raz ISBN: 978 — 0— 06— 240780— 1*

21. **Negotiation Genius — How to overcome obstacles and achieve brilliant results at the bargaining table and beyond.** *By Deepak Malhotra and Max H. Bazerman. eISBN: 978— 0— 55390494— 9*

22. **Getting (More Of) What You Want — How the secrets of economics and psychology can help you negotiate anything, in business and life.** *By Margaret A. Neale and Thomas Z. Lys ISBN: 978— 0— 465— 05072— 7 (hardcover) ISBN: 978— 0— 465— 04063— 6 (eBook)*

23. **Getting To Yes — Negotiating agreement without giving in.** *2nd Edition. By Roger Fisher, William Try and Bruce Patton. ISBN: 978— 0— 14— 015735— 2*

24. **Getting Past No — Negotiating in difficult situations.** *By William Try. eISBN: 978— 0— 55390364— 5*

25. **The Power Of Noticing — What the best leaders see.** *By Max H. Bazerman. ISBN: 978— 1— 4767— 0029— 8 (print book) ISBN: 978— 1— 47670031— 1 (eBook)*

26. **Can I Have Your Attention — How to think fast, find your focus and sharpen your concentration.** *By Joseph Cardillo. ISBN: 978— 1— 60163— 063— 6*

27. **The Sheikh CEO — Lessons in leadership from Mohammed Bin Rashid Al Maktoum.** *By Dr. Yasar Jarrar ISBN: 978— 1— 78596— 110— 6*

28. **Everything Is F*cked: A Book about Hope.** *By Mark Manson. ISBN: 978— 0062888433*

29. **Everything Is F*cked: A Book about Hope.** *By Mark Manson. ISBN: 978— 0062888433*

30. Download link to The Project Gutenberg eBook of A Message to Garcia, by Elbert Hubbard https://book.11ceohabits.com/bookfunnelgarcia

31. **3:59.4: The Quest to Break the 4 Minute Mile.** *By John Bryant ISBN: 978— 0099469087*

32. **Inside The Minds Of Healthcare Serial Killers — Why they kill.** *By Katherine Ramsland ISBN: 978— 0— 275— 99422— 8*

33. **One Hundred Years Of Medical Murder.** *By John Camp ISBN: 978— 0586056172*

34. **Undercover — How I went from company man to FBI spy and exposed the worst healthcare fraud in US history.** *By John W. Schilling. ISBN: 978— 1452055084*

35. **Secrets to Winning at Office Politics: How to Achieve Your Goals and Increase Your Influence at Work.** *By Marie G. McIntyre ISBN: 978-0312332181*

36. **Confessions of a Sociopath: A Life Spent Hiding in Plain Sight.** *By M.E. Thomas. ISBN: 978-0307956651*

37. **Becoming the Narcissist's Nightmare: How to Devalue and Discard the Narcissist While Supplying yourself.** *By Shahida Arabi. ISBN: 978-1523702466*
38. **Explaining Evil.** *By J. Harold Ellens. ISBN: 978-0313387159*
39. 11 CEO Habits - Wake Up The CEO Within You: The Ultimate Guide For Managers, Newbies And Interns. By Sukhdeep Sachdev. ISBN: 978— 1— 7357986— 7— 7

# THE BLOG LIST

1. Reference blog article A Man's Word Is His Bond — 4 Tips To Keep Your Promises http://book.11ceohabits.com/promises
2. Reference blog article How to Write an Elevator Pitch https://book.11ceohabits.com/zetypitch
3. Reference blog article 7 Comebacks to a Verbal Bully https://book.11ceohabits.com/verbalbully
4. Reference blog article Top Ten Clean Comebacks and Roasts https://book.11ceohabits.com/cleancomebacks
5. Reference blog article Top ten counter comebacks to other people's comebacks https://book.11ceohabits.com/replytocomebacks
6. 25 Funny Ways to Say NO https://book.11ceohabits.com/funnyno
7. Reference blog article Clear Communication is About Structure https://book.11ceohabits.com/communication
8. Reference blog article Speed as a Habit https://book.11ceohabits.com/speedhabit
9. Reference blog article 'Dealing with energy-sucking 'deadwood' employees https://book.11ceohabits.com/deadwood
10. Reference blog article 20 Diversion Tactics Highly Manipulative Narcissists, Sociopaths And Psychopaths Use To Silence You https://book.11ceohabits.com/tactics
11. Reference blog article 49 Secrets Your Boss Won't Tell You — But You Need to Know https://book.11ceohabits.com/secrets
12. Reference blog article 'Who are the World's Worst Tourists?' By Time Pile. https://book.11ceohabits.com/worsttourists
13. Khatri N., Tsang E.W.K. (2016) Antecedents and Consequences of Cronyism in Organizations. In: Khatri N., Ojha A.K. (eds) Crony Capitalism in India. Palgrave Studies in In-

dian Management. Palgrave Macmillan, London. https://book.11ceohabits.com/cronycapitalism

# THE VIDEO LIST

1. Reference video Change Blindness https://book.11ceohabits.com/changeblindness
2. Reference video The monkey Business Illusion https://book.11ceohabits.com/monkeybusiness
3. Reference video The 3 Types of Attention to Detail https://book.11ceohabits.com/attentionvideo
4. Reference video The Miracle Worker — Helen's First Lesson https://book.11ceohabits.com/miracleworker
5. Reference video Hillary Yip on Entrepreneurship https://book.11ceohabits.com/yiptips

# THE DOWNLOAD LIST

1. Download link to The Project Gutenberg eBook of A Message to Garcia, by Elbert Hubbard https://book.11ceohabits.com/bookfunnelgarcia

*The usual stuff …*

 Created with Vellum

Made in the USA
Monee, IL
09 March 2021

9e1ef393-90a4-42ed-bdf2-878e38978f80R01